Natural Los Angeles

Other books by Bill Thomas

The Island

The Swamp

American Rivers: A Natural History

How You Can Make $50,000 a Year As a Nature Photojournalist

Talking with the Animals: How to Communicate with Wildlife

The Brown County Book

Natural Washington

Natural New York

Natural Chicago

Indiana: Off the Beaten Path

Natural
Los Angeles

Bill Thomas

HARPER & ROW, PUBLISHERS, New York
Grand Rapids, Philadelphia, St. Louis, San Francisco
London, Singapore, Sydney, Tokyo

FIRST EDITION

Designed by Karen Savary

Maps by Karen Savary

Library of Congress Cataloging-in-Publication Data

Thomas, Bill, 1934–
  Natural Los Angeles/Bill Thomas.—1st ed.
    p. cm.
  Includes index.
  ISBN 0-06-055168-2 ISBN 0-06-096275-5 (pbk.)
  1. Los Angeles Region (Calif.)—Description and travel—Guidebooks. 2. Natural areas—California—Los Angeles Region—Guidebooks. 3. Los Angeles (Calif.)—Description—1981—Guidebooks. 4. Natural areas—California—Los Angeles—Guidebooks. I. Title.
F869.L83T48 1989
917.94′940453—dc19   88-45947

---

89 90 91 92 93 DT/FG 10 9 8 7 6 5 4 3 2 1
89 90 91 92 93 DT/FG 10 9 8 7 6 5 4 3 2 1 (pbk.)

This work is dedicated to friends of the natural environment—everywhere.

Contents

I: The Heartlands

II: East by Northeast

III: South by Southeast

Acknowledgments

Since the number of people who were helpful in compiling the materials for this volume far exceed what could be placed upon this page, I wish to collectively thank them and hope they will be as proud as I am of the book they helped to create.

A Note to the Reader

This work, which represents many months of effort by numerous people, is both a directory and a how-to book. It tells you not only about the natural areas of southern California, but also how to get there and where to obtain information. You must realize, of course, that many things are constantly changing. The natural areas described here will remain much the same, but if you find that routes of getting there have changed or that the addresses and phone numbers are different, keep in mind you may have to do some research on your own. I hope the extra effort will only add to the pleasure of your visit and enhance the value of this volume for you.

A Word About Personal Safety

Although most areas are relatively safe, it is my considered judgment that security comes best with caution. When you visit any natural area, be aware constantly of everything around you. If there are suspicious-looking people also visiting that area, keep your distance or come back another time. Some areas are safe during the day, but not as safe at dusk or after dark. Mornings are usually more safe than afternoons. Many natural areas and parks close at least from sunset to sunrise. There is also safety in numbers. Take someone with you when you visit natural areas; it's more fun and you can share your discoveries with others as well. Remember, the best defense is your own common sense. Take nothing for granted.

Remember, too, when visiting any natural area, take nothing but pictures and memories; leave nothing but footprints.

Introduction

No city in this hemisphere has a more varied natural environment close at hand than Los Angeles. Within a few hours' drive from the metropolitan area are snow-capped mountains cleft by deep canyons, dense woodlands, tumbling brooks, broad expanses of desert, towering sand dunes, the Pacific Ocean, wonderful beaches and fascinating tide pools, rocky sea islands, lush fern glens, meadows carpeted with wildflowers, tall-grass prairie.

Many rare and endangered wildlife species live within 100 miles of this sprawling metropolis. The California condor, one of the rarest birds in the world, is making its final stand in the Los Padres National Forest near Santa Barbara. On offshore Anacapa Island, brown pelicans have established their only West Coast nesting site. Elephant seals gather by the hundreds on San Miguel Island during winter months. Bald and golden eagles soar over canyons and chaparral all year, and mountain lions—though now few in number—still find sanctuary in mountainous terrain less than an hour's drive from downtown Los Angeles. The sparsely populated California desert is home to the reclusive desert tortoise.

One of the greatest wildlife spectacles anywhere is the annual migration of thousands of gray whales. On their way south from the Arctic to Baja California between Christmas and the end of February, they follow a route that lies about one-half mile from the southern California coast. Spectators, hoping to sight one or more of the great creatures, crowd shoreline observation points or join organized whale-watching expeditions that carry them offshore.

Plant life in southern California staggers the imagination. The chaparral—the nearly impenetrable brush that clings to much of the mountainous terrain

—is unique in North America. In the desert, forests of spectacular Joshua trees, members of the lily family that can grow up to 40 feet tall, lift grotesquely twisted arms to the sky. The official state flower is the California poppy, a golden-hued wildflower that opens it petals to the sun during the day and closes them at night. Among the sand dunes of the desert, the evening primrose flowers late in the afternoon; its blooms, white at first, turn pink before dying one day later. The bright yellow of the coreopsis, found along the coast and on offshore islands, is so brilliant that it can be seen by sailors miles out to sea on a clear day. If winter rains have been ample, the sand verbena, a creeper with stems that reach 3 feet in length, may carpet miles of desert with bright pink flowers. An oak tree in Encino, whose branches cover half a city block, is more than 1,000 years old, and in Santa Barbara, there's an enormous Moreton Bay fig tree that would fill half a football field.

Cultivated plants in the Los Angeles area come from all over the world. The state's first navel orange tree, brought here from Brazil in 1873, stands at the corner of Magnolia and Arlington streets in Riverside and still bears fruit.

The natural feature that is perhaps best known beyond the Golden State's borders is the San Andreas earthquake fault. In truth, the San Andreas is but one of many earthquake faults that underlie California. Shudders in the earth's surface occur almost daily, and earthquakes of destructive magnitude have taken place on an average of once a year for the past fifty years. There are places along fault lines where you may see rocks warped and bent by restless underground forces, land that has fractured and slipped, ponds that have formed in sagging depressions created when the earth shifted.

Five national forests; the Channel Islands National Park; the Santa Monica National Recreation Area; numerous state, county, and municipal parks; natural sanctuaries established and maintained by private organizations or individuals, holdings of The Nature Conservancy and the National Audubon Society; millions of acres of desert managed by the Bureau of Land Management; even military reservations—all are part of the natural landscape of southern California.

Its beauty and its Mediterranean climate have made southern California one of the most heavily populated spots in the world. Problems related to Los Angeles's overwhelming growth are many—the air is unhealthy to breathe a good part of the year, fresh water is both polluted and scarce, the pressures of life are enormous. Therefore, it is more important than ever to maintain open spaces where one can occasionally retreat, reevaluate life's priorities, and store up golden memories. As Thoreau said, "We need the tonic of wilderness. . . . We need to witness our own limits transgressed, and some life pasturing freely where we never wander."

It is our hope that this volume will help you to discover many quiet corners and to seek out others on your own. Space limitations do not permit us to include all such places that lie within the 100-mile radius covered by this book, but the sources of information listed throughout the text can often direct you to other areas of interest to nature lovers.

One final word—enjoy these places, but also respect and preserve them. Their worth to you and generations yet to come is incalculable.

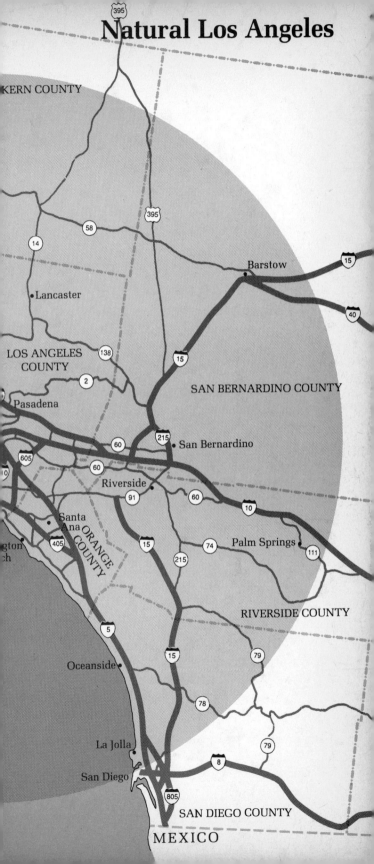

Natural Los Angeles

I

The Heartlands

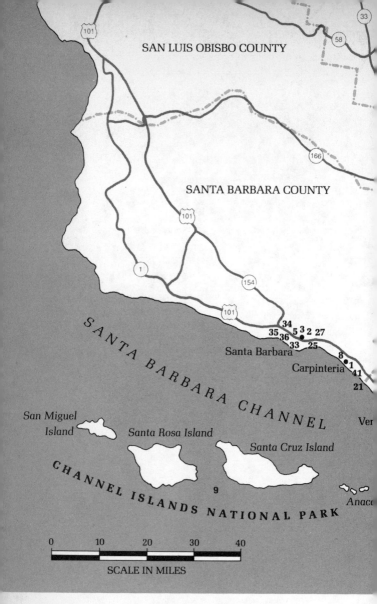

SAN LUIS OBISBO COUNTY

SANTA BARBARA COUNTY

SANTA BARBARA CHANNEL

Santa Barbara

Carpinteria

Ver

San Miguel Island

Santa Rosa Island

Santa Cruz Island

Anac

CHANNEL ISLANDS NATIONAL PARK

0   10   20   30   40

SCALE IN MILES

I: The Heartlands

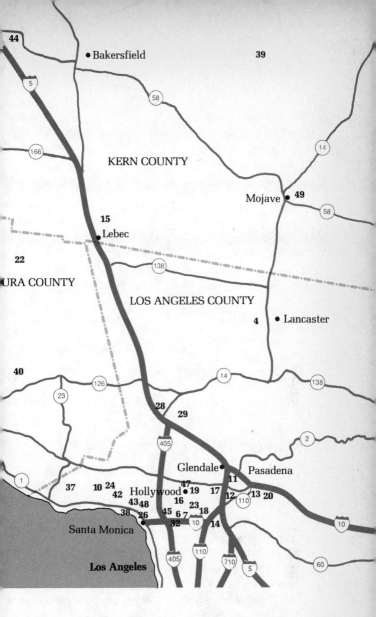

1. Abbey Garden Nursery

Located in the coastal town of Carpinteria is one of the finest cactus gardens in southern California. Some 1,700 species of succulents and cacti in a wide variety of forms may be seen here under one roof. Cactus flowers add gay splashes of vivid color.

How to Get There: From LA, drive north on U.S. 101 to Carpinteria. At the Linden Ave. exit, turn southwest to Carpinteria Ave.; then turn northwest (right) to the nursery.

Open 9–5 daily, except Thanksgiving and Christmas. Free. Free tours may be arranged in advance by phone.

For Additional Information:
Abbey Garden Nursery
4620 Carpinteria Ave.
Carpinteria, CA 93013

805-684-5112

2. Alameda Plaza

Trees are the featured attraction at Alameda Plaza in Santa Barbara. More than seventy species are found in this small park that covers just two square blocks. Among them are specimens from all over the world, including many that are rare. Most of the trees were brought here by a local resident in the early 1900s. Labels identify the different varieties.

Residents and visitors alike are drawn to this green oasis in the middle of town, where they may relax on benches beneath the spreading branches of tall trees. Adjoining the plaza is the Park Memorial Garden (described elsewhere).

Picnicking

Several picnic tables are scattered about the park. Children will enjoy the playground equipment.

How to Get There: From LA, drive north on U.S. 101 to Santa Barbara. At the Carillo St. exit, take Carillo St. northeast to Santa Barbara St. and turn northwest

(left) to plaza. Santa Barbara St. bisects Alameda Plaza between Sola and Micheltorena Sts. Parking on street.
    Open daily at all times. Free.

For Additional Information:
Parks Director
City of Santa Barbara
402 E. Ortega St.
Santa Barbara, CA 93101

805-963-0611

3. Andrée Clark Bird Refuge

Near the eastern edge of Santa Barbara is a small lagoon sprinkled with lush islets and edged by grassy shores. It is the heart of a 42-acre refuge that lures water birds by the thousands—mallard and shoveler ducks, coots, egrets, blue and green herons, sandpipers, and cormorants.
    The best time to see the birds in large numbers is late in the afternoon when they fly in from the ocean and settle down for the night, but the parklike surroundings are serene and beautiful any time of the day. Walkways and bicycle paths lead visitors along the water's edge and past well-tended gardens.

How to Get There: From LA, take U.S. 101 north to the Cabrillo Blvd. off ramp in Santa Barbara. Take Cabrillo Blvd. southwest to Los Patos Way and turn northwest. A small parking lot is located at the southwest corner of the intersection of Los Patos Way and the Southern Pacific Railroad tracks.
    Open daily, year-round, sunrise to sunset. Free.

For Additional Information:
Conference & Visitors Bureau
22 E. Anapamu St.
Santa Barbara, CA 93101

805-966-9222

Santa Barbara Zoological Gardens
500 Ninos Dr.
Santa Barbara, CA 93103

805-962-6310

4. Antelope Valley California Poppy Reserve

In 1977, the state of California set aside 1,745 acres near Lancaster and dedicated it to the state's official flower, the California poppy. Perched amid the gentle hills of the Antelope Valley on the western edge of the Mojave Desert, the reserve and surrounding lands are transformed each spring from subtle brown and green to glowing gold. Then the poppies spill their resplendent color across the land, creating a spectacle of beauty that lures thousands of visitors. Depending upon rainfall and temperature, the parade may begin as early as mid-March, but generally is at its best during the month of April.

There are other wildflowers, too—yellow goldfields and coreopsis, purple lupine and chia, white cream cups, and the violet redstem filarees—all blending together to weave a multihued tapestry of blossoms.

During the spring of 1982, the Jane S. Pinheiro Interpretive Center, located in the center of the reserve, was opened. Built with energy conservation in mind, the center is powered by a wind generator, heated by the sun, and insulated by the hillside it abuts. Exhibits of Antelope Valley flora and fauna place special emphasis on the California poppy and include a collection of wildflower paintings by the late Mrs. Pinheiro, who was the area's lay wildflower authority until her death in 1978.

Hiking and nature study are the primary activities here, and you may wander freely around the reserve, but keep an eye out for the several species of rattlesnakes that make their home here. During the period when they're emerging from hibernation, which usually coincides with the spring poppy extravaganza, they are sluggish and grumpy.

The entire Antelope Valley is famous for its masses of spring wildflowers. Each year, for about a month during the peak of the blooming season, the Lancaster Chamber of Commerce opens a special Wildflower Center at 841 West Avenue J in Lancaster. Maps of the best viewing areas are provided at no charge, and flower seeds may be purchased.

Although this area is most popular when the wildflowers are in bloom, it is an interesting place to observe throughout the year. Antelope Valley, located

2,000 to 3,000 feet above sea level, is a windswept land of far-reaching horizons and temperature extremes. Except for an occasional Joshua tree, it seems more pastoral than desertlike. Plants from the coastal hills and central valley intermingle with the flora of the desert.

How to Get There: From LA, go north on I-5 to CA 14 (Antelope Valley Fwy.) and turn northeast. Follow CA 14 to the Ave. I exit in Lancaster and turn west. The poppy reserve lies about 15 miles west of Lancaster on both sides of Ave. I. The entrance gate and Pinheiro Center are on the north (right) side of the highway.

   Reserve lands are open daily, year-round, from ½ hour before sunrise to ½ hour after sunset. Center, roads, and parking areas open daily, year-round, 8–4:30. Free.

For Additional Information:
Manager
High Desert Area Office
California Department of Parks & Recreation
43066 N. 10th Street
Lancaster, CA 93534

805-945-9173

Lancaster Chamber of Commerce
44943 Tenth St. West
Lancaster, CA 93534

805-948-4518

Antelope Valley California Poppy Preserve
Department of Parks & Recreation
15101 W. Lancaster Rd.
Lancaster, CA 93534

805-945-7811

Poppy Preserve Interpretative Association
4555 W. Ave. G.
Lancaster, CA 93534

(no phone)

5. Arroyo Burro Beach County Park

Among the attractions of this 6-acre park are a sandy beach, numerous tide pools, and a sweeping view of the Santa Barbara Channel. Arroyo Burro, the small stream for which the park is named, spills into the ocean near the park's eastern boundary. The coastal chapparal that blankets much of the landscape includes sages, native sun, and poison oak. During winter months, migrating whales may be sighted from the bluffs above the beach, and in the spring, there are wildflowers galore at the west end of the park. Beachcombers scan the shoreline for onyx and petrified whalebone. Visitors will also find limited hiking and equestrian trails.

Fishing

Surf and spear fishermen catch such species as halibut, bonito, mackerel, barracuda, calico bass, and white sea bass. A bait and tackle shop is located in the park.

Swimming, Skin and Scuba Diving, and Surfing

A swimming beach edges 600 feet of shoreline. Dressing rooms are available, and during summer months, a lifeguard is on duty. Snorkelers and scuba divers enjoy exploring the kelp beds that lie just offshore, and surfers ride some of the best waves in the area.

Picnicking

A small family picnic area is located in a grassy field with a snack bar nearby.

How to Get There: From LA, take U.S. 101 north and west to Las Positas Rd. (CA 225) on the west side of Santa Barbara. Turn south to Cliff Dr., then west ½ mile to the park entrance on the south side of the road. Parking on site.

Open daily, year-round, during daylight hours. Free.

For Additional Information:
Director of Parks
Santa Barbara County Parks Department
2981 Cliff Dr.
Santa Barbara, CA 93109

805-687-3714 (park)

6. Beverly Gardens Park

A local landmark since it was conceived in the 1930s, this linear green space runs through the heart of Beverly Hills. Visitors may stroll or jog along a 2-mile gravel path for a close-up look at the park's flora. In addition to an extensive rose garden, several unusual trees, ornamental fountains, and a lily pond, there's an extraordinary Cactus Garden filled with specimen cacti and succulents gathered from all over the world.

How to Get There: From LA, go north on U.S. 101 to Santa Monica Blvd. and turn west to Beverly Hills. The narrow strip of parkland borders the north side of Santa Monica Blvd. between Doheny Dr. and Wilshire Blvd., then continues along the north side of Wilshire Blvd. to Whittier Dr. The park's main attraction, its Cactus Garden, lies along Santa Monica Blvd. between Camden and Bedford drs. Parking available on several cross streets.

Open daily at all times. Free.

For Additional Information:
Beverly Hills Visitors Bureau
239 S. Beverly Dr.
Beverly Hills, CA 90212

213-271-8174 or 800-345-2210

Beverly Hills Recreation & Parks Department
450 N. Crescent Dr.
Beverly Hills, CA 90210

213-550-4864

7. California Natural History Tours

For those who do not wish to plan their own journeys, California Natural History Tours will take you to many of the locations mentioned in this directory. They also travel to other outstanding places such as Big Sur, Death Valley, the bristlecone pine country, the Owen Valley, and into Baja for the whale migration. Tours are generally led by a naturalist expert in the field or subject matter for that particular tour.

How to Contact: The tour office is located in Beverly Hills, but you should call or write California Natural History Tours at the address given below.
  Open daily.

For Additional Information:
California Natural History Tours
P.O. Box 3709
Beverly Hills, CA 90212
213-274-3025

8. Carpinteria State Beach

Although it's just 50 acres in size, Carpinteria State Beach offers more than many larger beaches. The Santa Ynez Mountains form a scenic backdrop for the narrow, curving beach, and the Pacific Ocean laps at its doorstep. At its western end, the beach is bordered by a 20-foot bluff and to the east by low sand dunes. There are some fascinating tide pools along the shoreline, and beachcombers consider this one of the best spots in which to scout for shells and pebbles. Occasionally, glass floats from fishermen's nets will wash ashore. Seals and sea lions are sometimes spotted on offshore rocks.

Camping

More than 250 campsites accommodate tents and recreational vehicles; showers, tables, fire pits, several complete hookups, disposal station.

Water Sports

Carpinteria is known as the "safest beach on the coast" because a reef 2,000 feet out eliminates surf; lifeguard on duty during the summer. An area called the "tar pits" at the south end of the beach is popular with surfers.
  Surf fishermen catch perch, corbina, bass, and cabezon.

How to Get There: The beach is surrounded by the city of Carpinteria in Santa Barbara County. From LA, take U.S. 101 northwest to the Casitas Pass exit in Carpinteria, then take Casitas Pass south toward the beach. At Carpinteria Ave., turn west (right) and proceed to Palm Ave. Turn south (left) onto Palm Ave. Follow this street to its terminus at the state beach. Parking on site.

Open 7 A.M.–9 P.M. from the last Sunday in April to the last Sunday in October; open the rest of the year 7 A.M.–5 P.M. Vehicle admission fee.

For Additional Information:
Carpinteria State Beach
361 6th St.
Carpinteria, CA 93013

805-684-2811

California Department of Parks & Recreation
Channel Coast Area
24 E. Main St.
Ventura, CA 93001

805-654-4611

9. Channel Islands National Park

Lying 10 to 70 miles off the southern California coastline are five islands known collectively as the Channel Islands National Park. The four northern islands —Anacapa, San Miguel, Santa Cruz, and Santa Rosa —march westward single file toward the open sea. The fifth, Santa Barbara, lies approximately 40 miles to the south. Together, they make up one of the Golden State's premier wilderness areas, a unique and magical place sculpted by sea and wind where it is still possible to experience silent moments.

The waters, too, are protected here. The area within 1 nautical mile of the shorelines of Anacapa, San Miguel, and Santa Barbara islands is maintained as a California State Ecological Reserve. Beyond that, to a distance of 6 nautical miles from the shorelines of each of these islands, and for 6 nautical miles from the shorelines of Santa Rosa and Santa Cruz islands, lies the Channel Islands National Marine Sanctuary.

Because of their isolation and because they are situated at a point in the Pacific where the cold waters of the north blend with the warm waters of the south, the park, reserve, and sanctuary shelter one of the most diversified and productive marine ecosystems in the world, including many life forms that exist nowhere else on earth. More than sixty species of birds nest and feed in and around the islands. Each year, from about November to April, an estimated 15,000 California gray whales pass through this area on their annual migration between Alaska and Mexico. Seals and sea lions can be seen on beaches and rocky ledges, and the endangered sea otter is making a comeback here. Occasionally, great white and blue sharks slip quietly through vast underwater forests of kelp. The rare and exquisite California hydrocoral thrives in abundance in the shallow waters close to the islands. At low tide, you can explore colorful tide pools that flourish in a million niches.

Archaeological digs have revealed some of the oldest traces of man on the North American continent, and a geologic history that began some 14 million years ago is etched in the faces of rock cliffs.

Visually, the islands are stunning, the last vestiges of a southern California that once was and can never be again. The landscape is primeval—wild and free. Fog-draped mountaintops plunge to meet precipitous cliffs at the water's edge, and deep sea caves whisper of secrets hidden for centuries. In late summer and autumn, the land is dusky brown. Then come the winter rains and a metamorphosis to lush green. Wildflowers, many extremely rare, some found only on these islands, splash vivid colors across an emerald carpet of grass in spring and early summer.

Before visiting the islands themselves, stop in at the park's mainland Visitor Center in Ventura. There are few facilities on the islands themselves, and you'll find it well worth your while to learn something of each island's special features before visiting them.

Although all five islands described here lie within park boundaries, Santa Cruz and Santa Rosa remain private property at this writing. The federal government, however, has options to buy certain portions of Santa Cruz and all of Santa Rosa in the future. To the south of the park are three more islands that are part of the Channel Islands chain. Santa Catalina (described elsewhere) is the only one of the three accessible to the public; San Nicolas and San Clemente are administered by the U.S. Navy as missile tracking stations and bombing ranges.

Anacapa Island

The island closest to the mainland and therefore the most accessible, Anacapa is located approximately 11 miles south of Oxnard. Actually a chain of three separate islets linked by reefs, this small, narrow archipelago totals some 700 acres and extends to a length of 5 miles. In spring, Anacapa is a mass of shimmering gold. It is then that the island's most distinctive plant, the giant coreopsis or tree sunflower, blankets the terrain with bright blooms that on a clear day can be seen 10 miles out to sea. The endangered brown pelican nests on West Anacapa, which is off-limits unless you obtain written permission to land from the park superintendent. At one end of East Anacapa, a U.S. Coast Guard lighthouse sounds its foghorn every thirteen seconds, day and night. Anacapa is also one of the best spots from which to watch the California gray whales during their annual migration from about November to April. At any time of the year, you'll see myriads of birds, including western gulls, black oystercatchers, double-breasted cormorants, and scoter ducks.

Anacapa Island

San Miguel Island

The westernmost of the Channel Islands, and therefore the least protected from the elements, San Miguel
is battered relentlessly by wind and wave. More species of pinnipeds are found on this 9,000-acre island
than in any other single location in the world. The
California sea lion, northern fur seal, northern elephant seal, Steller's sea lion, and harbor seal have
established breeding colonies here, and the endangered Guadalupe fur seal suns on sandy beaches.
Great dunes are shifted and reshaped by the wind,
revealing a unique "caliche forest" of stark, gray limestone pillars. To form them, organic acids in living
plants and sand interacted to encase the vegetation in
a stone sheath. The plants have long since rotted
away, creating a striking and unusual natural wonder.

Santa Cruz Island

Lovely Santa Cruz is regarded as the crown jewel of
the Channel Islands, a rare remnant of primeval
America just 24 miles from the City of Santa Barbara.
Comprised of 62,000 acres, it is California's largest
offshore island. Its 77 miles of shoreline include
cliffs, coves, sandy beaches, bays, and more than 100
known sea caves, the most noted of which is the
cathedral-like Painted Cave with a 70-foot-high ocean
entrance and multicolored walls stained by mineral
oxides. Several of the island's interior mountain
peaks soar skyward more than 1,700 feet; the loftiest
reaches more than 2,400 feet. There are steep canyons, dense woods, streams fed by freshwater springs,
and open meadows. Of the more than 600 species of
plants found on the island, about forty are restricted
to the Channel Islands and eight occur only on Santa
Cruz. Hundreds of seals and sea lions haul out on the
beaches and rocky ledges and feed in azure waters
rich with marine life. Just offshore are vast forests of
kelp, tall seaweed "trees" that waver with every
movement of the water, where thousands of fish dart
about. Scientists estimate that there are approximately 3,000 significant archaeological sites on the
island. The Nature Conservancy, a national conservation organization, recently purchased the western
nine tenths of Santa Cruz, assuring the preservation

of that portion of the island. As part of the sale terms, the former owner, a cattle rancher who operates under the name of the Santa Cruz Island Company, will retain lifetime occupancy rights. The remaining one-tenth, still privately owned and operated as a sheep ranch by the Gherini family, will eventually be purchased by the federal government. However, visitors are welcome on the entire island if they make arrangements in advance through the ranchers or join one of the frequent tour groups.

Santa Rosa Island

The second largest of the park's islands, Santa Rosa covers approximately 53,000 acres. Its 45-mile shoreline varies from inviting beaches, bright spits of white sand, and 400-foot-high dunes to craggy bluffs riddled with sea caves. Inland, the terrain climbs to a high point of nearly 1,600 feet. A huge split in the earth, tucked away among the mountains, is the legacy of a

Elephant seals on San Miguel Island

violent 1812 earthquake. Although all four northern
Channel Islands have yielded important archaeological data, Santa Rosa is particularly rich in such sites.
A recent find here indicates the presence of man more
than 40,000 years ago, about 30,000 years earlier than
Homo sapiens was previously believed to have been
in North America. One of only two known stands of
Torrey pines in the world grows on this island (the
other is near San Diego at Torrey Pines State Reserve,
described elsewhere), along with more than 350 other
types of plants. Among the multitude of wildlife that
lives on the island are some imported deer and elk; a
native Island fox, no larger than a house cat; wild
boar; and spotted skunks. Santa Rosa is currently
owned by the Vail and Vickers Cattle Ranch. In the
future, the island will be purchased by the federal
government, but until then you must contact the owners for permission to visit.

Santa Barbara Island

Santa Barbara, the smallest of the Channel Islands
within the national park, covers just 1 square mile.
Nonetheless, it is a majestic, intriguing place edged
by cliffs that climb as high as 500 feet. There are fantastic tide pools and sea caves to explore, and numerous blowholes add a touch of drama. Although this
island was farmed in the past, native vegetation is
beginning to make a comeback. The only known specimens of the Santa Barbara live-forever, a plant once
thought to be extinct, grow on an inaccessible cliff.
California sea lions and harbor seals crowd the rocky
shoreline, and northern elephant seals breed here in
the winter. In contrast to its ruggedness at the water's
edge, the island is topped by a flat, gentle meadow
that affords sweeping views of the horizon, one more
spectacular than the next. Each spring, western gulls
nest among the tall grasses.

Hiking

Santa Barbara has perhaps the best trail system of all
the islands in the national park. Canyon View Nature
Trail, a quarter-mile loop with a self-guiding brochure, offers a variety that hints at what you'll see
elsewhere on the island. Other trails lead past giant

coreopsis thickets to a small battery-powered light-house and to lookouts that provide good views of California sea lions and elephant seals.

A 1¼-mile-long nature trail on East Anacapa follows a figure-eight pattern. Stay away from the light-house, however; the high-intensity foghorn can permanently damage your ears. If arrangements are made in advance, the resident ranger will conduct tours, walks, and other programs for groups.

San Miguel Island offers a trail nearly 8 miles long from Cuyler Harbor to Point Bennett, a favorite gathering place for thousands of seals and sea lions. Before visiting here, be sure to pick up a free permit in advance at national park headquarters in Ventura.

In addition, there are many trails of varying lengths to follow on both Santa Cruz and Santa Rosa, the two largest islands. These trails are not maintained, however.

A word of caution—stay away from the cliffs. They'll crumble in places. Also, be prepared for some steep climbs.

Boating and Fishing

Most visitors to the Channel Islands get there by commercial boat services, but many like to use their own boats. First-time visitors should check at the park headquarters/Visitor Center in Ventura for pertinent information. Since there are no private docks available to individual boaters, you'll need a small boat or skiff to go ashore and explore the sea caves. Always keep in mind that sea and wind conditions in the Santa Barbara Channel are very unpredictable, especially in the afternoon. Only the most experienced boaters with sturdy vessels should attempt the trip to San Miguel, where the sea is usually rough. U.S. Coast Guard and Geodetic Survey Charts 18720, 18729, and 18756 provide navigation data for the waters surrounding park islands.

Fish caught by anglers and divers include rockfish, sheepshead, sand dabs, perch, abalone, scallops, and oysters. Since the waters around each island are very carefully managed and since regulations sometimes change, it's best to check current information and rules with park personnel.

Swimming, Snorkeling, and Scuba Diving

Beach swimming is available, on calm summer days, at Landing Cover on East Anacapa, at Frenchy's Cove in the break between Middle and West Anacapa, in the many well-protected coves along the north shore of Santa Cruz, and at several points on San Miguel.

Snorkeling and scuba diving around the islands are extremely popular. The sunlight filtering through a lush, 60-foot-deep forest of kelp that moves sinuously with every surge of the sea, combined with the startling colors of the thousands of fish who feed there, creates an unforgettable underwater panorama. There are also many shipwrecks to explore.

Camping

Free primitive tent camping is permitted on Anacapa and Santa Barbara islands. Campers must bring all supplies, including drinking water, with them. Since there are so few campsites, reservations are necessary and should be made at least two weeks in advance; contact park headquarters in Ventura.

Picnicking

There are no facilities on the islands, but you're welcome to bring along a picnic lunch and eat wherever you choose.

How to Get There: You may drive to the park's Visitor Center on the mainland, but the islands are accessible only by boat.

To reach the Visitor Center, take U.S. 101 north from LA toward Ventura. Just before reaching Ventura, turn south at the Victoria Ave. exit. Follow Victoria Ave. to Olivas Park Dr. and turn west. Olivas Park Dr. will lead you to the Visitor Center, but will change names along the way. After crossing over Harbor Blvd., Olivas Park Dr. becomes Spinnaker Dr. When you reach the beach, Spinnaker veers to the right and becomes Shoreline Dr. Shoreline Dr. ends at the waterfront visitor center. There are many signs along the way. Open daily, year-round, 8–5 Monday–Friday; 8:30–5 Saturday and Sunday.

To reach the islands, most visitors choose to join organized tours or expeditions. These usually originate from Santa Barbara, Ventura, or Carpinteria. You may take a day cruise or overnight camping trips of various lengths. Some day cruises circle the islands; others take you ashore for a few hours. A few cruises offer the option of free navigation and sailing instructions during your trip. Special charters are available year-round. Many museums and organizations in southern California include natural history tours of one or more of the Channel Islands as part of their annual field trip schedules (see California Natural History Tours, described elsewhere). In general, tours are run more often during spring and summer months, but the winter whale migration is one of the most exciting times of all. Island Packers Co. (P.O. Box 993, Ventura, CA 93002; phone 805-642-1393) offers a diversity of tours on a regular basis and is also available for individual or group charters to any of the islands. For the names of additional tour operators and up-to-date transportation information, contact park headquarters.

Twice each month, The Nature Conservancy hosts naturalist-led day trips to Santa Cruz Island for the general public (minimum age ten years). For more information, contact Santa Cruz Island Project, c/o The Nature Conservancy, 735 State St., Suite 201, Santa Barbara, CA 93101 (phone 805-962-9111).

You may also take your own boat or charter one from any of a number of rental or charter locations along the southern California coast. The mainland cities closest to Anacapa, Santa Cruz, Santa Rosa, and San Miguel are Ventura and Santa Barbara. Anacapa, closest to the mainland, lies approximately 11 nautical miles west of Ventura, while San Miguel, furthest out to sea, is about 38 nautical miles southwest of Santa Barbara. Santa Barbara Island lies 38 miles west of San Pedro Harbor in Los Angeles. Plan to anchor offshore and take a small boat or skiff to land on each island. No permit is required to land on Anacapa or Santa Barbara. To obtain a permit for San Miguel, contact park headquarters. For Santa Rosa, contact Vail and Vickers, 123 W. Padre St., Santa Barbara, CA 93105 (phone 805-682-7645). For the western nine tenths of Santa Cruz, contact Santa Cruz Island Company, 515 S. Flower St., Los Angeles, CA 90071 (phone 213-485-9208); for the eastern tenth, contact Mr. Pier Gherini, 1114 State St. #230, Santa Barbara, CA 93101 (phone 805-966-4155) or Mr. Francis Gherini, 162 S. A St., Oxnard, CA 93030 (phone 805-483-8022).

For Additional Information:
Superintendent
Channel Islands National Park
1901 Spinnaker Dr.
Ventura, CA 93001

805-644-8157

10. Cold Creek Canyon Preserve

One of the most fascinating areas within the boundaries of the Santa Monica Mountains National Recreation Area (described elsewhere) is Cold Creek Canyon
Preserve, owned by The Nature Conservancy. Containing some 560 acres, the preserve not only has interesting geological features, but is a botanical
paradise. The rich diversity of the vegetation is due
primarily to the variety of natural features found here,
ranging from a year-round stream that is the last free-
flowing creek in Los Angeles County to dry, rocky
ridges.

Nine freshwater springs feed Cold Creek, and several waterfalls are formed as the creek makes its way
through the canyon. Wind caves share the hillsides
with patches of scrub oak, manzanita, and the rare
red shank. In the moist bottomlands, you'll see sycamores, willows, coast live oaks, and, unusual in this
region, two big-leaf maples. Several flowering ash
trees, which commonly reach a maximum height of
20 feet, grow 40 feet tall in this pristine environment.
Depending on the season, there will be a profusion of
wildflowers to see—orange monkey flowers, red California fuschia, purple nightshade, yellow Canyon
sunflowers, white or blue Ceanothus, and purple lupine.

Mule deer, coyote, bobcat, and rattlesnakes inhabit
the area, but are rarely sighted by visitors.

Hiking

A printed trail guide is available for a ¾-mile-long,
self-guided nature trail. The path is rugged, narrow,
slippery after a rain, and drops some 400 feet in elevation. At the end, you must return the way you came.
You can also explore other parts of the preserve via
an additional 2 miles of trails. Keep an eye out for the

poison oak that thrives here. Free guided nature walks are sometimes scheduled.

How to Get There: Located in western Los Angeles County northeast of Malibu. From LA, go north and west on U.S. 101 to Las Virgines–Malibu Canyon Rd. (Co. Hwy. N-1). Turn south to Mulholland Hwy., then east to Stunt Rd., then south to preserve entrance on east side of road. Park along Stunt Rd.

Open daily, year-round, sunrise to sunset. Free, but visitors must apply in advance for a permit or join a guided nature walk.

For Additional Information:
The Nature Conservancy
Southern California Chapter Project Office
213 Stearns Wharf
Santa Barbara, CA 93101

805-962-9111

The Nature Conservancy
California Field Office
785 Market St.
San Francisco, CA 94103

415-777-0487

Information Specialist
Santa Monica Mountains National Recreation Area
22900 Ventura Blvd.
Woodland Hills, CA 91364

818-888-3770

11. Descanso Gardens

Planted in the early 1930s when these grounds were part of a private estate, the world-renowned camellias of Descanso now stand more than 20 feet tall. Over 100,000 of these shade-loving plants grow beneath the leafy branches of ancient California oaks in an area known as the Camellia Forest. From November to March, the woodland glows with their brilliant blossoms, and paths through the forest are strewn with their petals.

A historical rose garden contains many unusual rose varieties that were popular during different periods of history, including some that date back to 1,200 B.C., while a modern rose garden nearby is devoted to All-American rose selections. Blooms may be seen from May through December.

No matter when you visit here, something will be in flower. Lilacs, azaleas, irises, orchids, rhododendrons, daffodils, begonias, fuschias, and chrysanthemums color the landscape at one time or another throughout the year. Cacti and succulents flourish in a garden devoted to the native plants of California. One of the loveliest areas of all is a fern grove, lush and luminous with varying hues of green.

Five species of hummingbirds live here, as does the Cooper's hawk, and the osprey is a winter visitor. From a unique observation station, you can watch wild ducks swimming on a small lake. Nature trails lead deep into woods where crystal-clear streams, fed by mountain springs, wander past a profusion of oaks, ginkgos, sycamores, pines, and giant redwoods.

A snack bar and gift shop are located on the premises, and you can enjoy tea and cookies at an authentic Japanese teahouse.

The entire property is maintained by the Los Angeles County Department of Arboreta and Botanic Gardens as an environmental study area.

How to Get There: Located in Los Angeles County, a few miles northeast of downtown LA. From LA, drive north on I-5 to CA 2 (Glendale Fwy.), then take CA 2 northeast to Foothill Blvd. Go east on Foothill Blvd. to Descanso Dr. and turn south to the gardens on the right side of the road. There are signs along the way. Parking on site.

Gardens open 9–4:30 daily, year-round; closed Christmas. Teahouse open 11–4 daily, March through Labor Day; Tuesday–Sunday the rest of the year. Nominal admission fee; free admission the third Tuesday of each month. Tram tours available 1-3 Tuesday–Friday, 11–4 Saturday, Sunday, and holidays.

For Additional Information:
Descanso Gardens
1418 Descanso Dr.
La Canada, CA 91011
818-790-5571

12. Eagle Rock

This massive, 150-foot-high sandstone rock owes its name to a natural formation imprinted on its southwest face. Best seen at noon, when shadows fall directly downward, the formation bears a remarkable likeness to an eagle with outstretched wings. Eagle Rock has been called Los Angeles's most distinctive natural landmark.

How to Get There: Located at the north end of Figueroa St., near the City of Los Angeles/City of Glendale boundary line. From LA, go north on I-5 to CA 2 (Glendale Pkwy.); take CA 2 northeast to CA 134 (Ventura Fwy.) and turn east. As you travel east from Glendale to Pasadena, you can see the rock formation on the north side of CA 134 near the Figueroa St. exit.

For Additional Information:
Greater Los Angeles Visitors & Convention Bureau
515 S. Figueroa St.
Los Angeles, CA 90071

213-689-8822

Glendale Chamber of Commerce
200 S. Louise St.
Glendale, CA 91205

213-240-7870

13. Elysian Park

Elysian Park rambles over 600 acres of forested hills and verdant valleys adjacent to Dodger Stadium. The two are worlds apart—one filled with noise and excitement, the other a quiet and serene natural sanctuary. Although seven miles of roads wander through the park, there are corners so remote that the only sound you'll hear is a symphony of birdsong.

Los Angeles's first arboretum is here. Begun in 1893 with three flowering coral trees, the 10-acre grove of rare specimens (some with labels) borders Stadium Way from Soctt Avenue on the south to the upper end of Chavez Ravine, where Stadium Way meets Elysian Park Drive on the north. Among the exotic trees seen here today is the only known golden-leaf Baphia in the nation. In recent years, planting has been resumed in the upper end of the arboretum and the city has made additional land available for a grove of unusual flowering trees.

The Los Angeles Police Academy's training center, built on land leased from the city in Elysian Park, contains a lovely rock garden with a series of cascades and pools that's open to the public. Also on the academy's grounds, located at 1880 Academy Dr., is a small café that serves reasonably priced meals from 7 A.M.–3:30 P.M. on weekdays.

Sports facilities include tennis courts, baseball diamonds, and, at the park's recreation center at 929 Academy Rd., volleyball and basketball courts.

Hiking

More than 10 miles of hiking trails lead through shady glens, up and down wooded hills, over grassy meadows, and to some spectacular views.

Picnicking

There are fifteen pleasant picnic areas in the park. Some tables are beneath imported rubber trees; others are under native oaks. Several areas along Stadium Way are equipped with grills.

How to Get There: Located west of the intersection of I-5 and CA 110. From downtown LA, go northeast on CA 110 (called Pasadena Fwy. north of U.S. 101) to the Stadium Way off ramp. Follow Stadium Way west and north into the park. Parking on site.

Park and recreation center open 6 A.M.–10 P.M. daily, year-round. Free.

For Additional Information:
City of Los Angeles Department of Recreation
   & Parks
200 N. Main St., 13th Floor
Los Angeles, CA 90012

213-485-5515

Griffith Park Ranger Station
4730 Crystal Springs Dr.
Los Angeles, CA 90027

213-665-5188

14. Exposition Park

Exposition Park near downtown Los Angeles is a mix of city, county, and state facilities. Its 7-acre sunken rose garden, which contains 16,000 bushes representing more than 190 varieties, is one of the most popular parts of the Los Angeles city park system. Though bright with multicolored blossoms about nine months of the year, the garden is in its prime in May and June. Some 2,000 visitors daily come to wander the grassy pathways and observe such species as the Jolly Roger, a coral floribunda; the Arizona, a two-tone peach and fuschia floribunda; the purple Paradise; the Bon-Bon, with pale red center and creamy white petals; and the bright-red Mister Lincoln, noted for its unusual perfume. Small markers identify each plant for you. At the center of the garden, lilies and water hyacinths dot the surface of a small pond.

The Natural History Museum of Los Angeles County, located just west of the rose garden, is the largest museum of its kind west of the Mississippi. Inside, you'll find more than thirty-five halls and galleries that contain collections of fossils, wildlife in simulated natural habitats, and artifacts of various cultures. An outstanding display of minerals and gems includes a huge amethyst geode, some rare gold crystals and Konigsberg silver, the world's finest public collection of colored sapphires, a 34-ounce gold nugget, some flawless emeralds, and a sample of tanzanite, a gem whose existence was first discovered in 1967. Allow some time to browse through the gift and book stores; a low-cost cafeteria is open 10–4:30. The museum also enlists amateurs to work, at their own expense, as field associates on digs or as lab technicians (phone 213-744-3310 on weekdays).

Nearby is the fascinating Museum of Science and Industry, one of the state's major educational facilities, where you can watch baby chicks hatch before your eyes. The park is also home to a Space Museum, full of air and space equipment on loan from such places as NASA; the open-air Los Angeles Memorial Coliseum, which hosted Olympic events in 1932 and 1984; the Memorial Sports Arena, an indoor sports and entertainment facility; and the Los Angeles Swimming Stadium, open to the public during summer months when no competitions are scheduled.

How to Get There: Located just south of downtown
LA. Go south on I-110 (Harbor Fwy.) to the Exposition Blvd. exit and go west for about two blocks. The
park is located on the south side of the street at 900
Exposition Blvd. (opposite the University of Southern
California), between Figueroa St. on the east and
Menlo Ave. on the west; Santa Barbara Ave. forms the
park's southern boundary. Parking on site (free except
on Coliseum event days).

Park open daily at all times. Free. Rose garden open
8:30–5 daily (from December–February, when roses
are not in bloom, the garden may be closed while the
staff is pruning). Free. Natural History Museum open
10–5, Tuesday–Sunday; closed January 1, Thanksgiving, December 25. Nominal admission fee, under 5
free, free to everyone the first Tuesday of each month.

For Additional Information:
City of Los Angeles Department of Recreation
  & Parks
200 N. Main St., 13th Floor
Los Angeles, CA 90012

213-485-5515

Natural History Museum of Los Angeles County
900 Exposition Blvd.
Los Angeles, CA 90007

213-744-DINO

15. Fort Tejon State Historic Park

Fort Tejon, established in 1854 as a U.S. Army post,
was described thus by an early visitor: "The post of
Tejon is on a little plain, entirely surrounded by high
mountains, beautifully situated in a grove of old oak
. . . On the plains and mountain sides, Mother Nature
has almost excelled herself, carpeting them with flowers of every hue . . . An oasis in the desert where all
is freshness and life."

Despite a disastrous earthquake in 1857 and the
construction of I-5 virtually at its doorstep, Fort Tejon
remains much the same today. It has been restored for
its historical value, but should be prized for its natural qualities as well. Many of the huge old oaks are
still there, including one that measures 8 feet in di-

ameter. A small stream that trickles by near the park's entrance is edged by black willows and cottonwoods. Sycamores shade the meadows, and in the spring, the fields are bright with the golden blooms of California poppies. Approximately four of the park's 204 acres have been set aside as a preserve for the rare Fort Tejon salamander. Black-tailed deer, beechey ground squirrels, bobcats, badger, gray foxes, and coyotes find refuge here, and occasionally a California condor, one of North America's most endangered birds, can be spotted riding the thermals overhead.

From 1857 to 1861, Fort Tejon served as the western terminus for the U.S. Camel Corps, which, under the direction of Jefferson Davis (former U.S. secretary of war and then president of the Confederacy), experimented with the use of camels as pack animals. The camels performed splendidly, but were no longer needed when railroads appeared on the scene.

Three earthquake monitoring stations in the park constantly check the activities of several major faults that pass through the area. Three buildings—the orderlies' quarters, officers' quarters, and some barracks —and exhibits at the Visitor Center reflect the lifestyle of the fort during its active years (1854–1864). On certain Sundays each summer (usually the third Sundays of June through October) mock Civil War battles are staged in the park at 11 A.M. and again at 1 and 3 P.M.

Hiking

Although there are no established trails, you may roam the mountainous backcountry of Fort Tejon Park at will. Elevations in the park range from 3,250 feet to 4,500 feet above sea level.

Picnicking

Several picnic tables are located on grassy lawns beneath giant shade trees and near the bank of the stream. Restrooms and drinking water are close at hand.

How to Get There: Located in southernmost Kern County. From LA, take I-5 north. About 3 miles after you pass Lebec, you'll see the Fort Tejon turnoff. The park is on the west side of the highway. Parking on site.

Park open daily, year-round, during daylight hours; buildings open 10–5, closed January 1, Thanksgiving, and December 25. Nominal admission fee.

For Additional Information:
Fort Tejon State Historic Park
Box 895
Lebec, CA 83243

805-248-6692

California Department of Parks & Recreation
South Valley Area
Rt. 1, Box 42
Buttonwillow, CA 93206

805-265-5004

16. Greystone Park

One of the most beautiful spots in Beverly Hills, remote from all the hoopla and glitter, is peaceful Greystone Park. Once it was part of a 400-acre ranch and home to the son of wealthy oilman Edward L. Doheny.

The gray stone façade and concrete-reinforced slate roof of its hilltop mansion give the park its name. Built between 1925 and 1928 at a cost of $4 million, the 55-room mansion has been featured in many films and television shows. It is generally regarded as the second most opulent residence ever constructed west of the Mississippi River (second only to William Randolph Hearst's San Simeon). In 1975, the cost to duplicate Greystone Mansion was estimated at nearly $80 million.

The grounds, as lovely as the home they were meant to complement, contain formal gardens, orchards, fountains, reflecting pools, ponds adorned with water lilies, lotus, and hibiscus; woods growing wild; and sweeping lawns that invite you to sit a spell. More than 100 plant species, brought here from all over the world, have identification markers close by. Walkways wander past avocado trees, redwoods, Victorian box trees, eucalyptus, evergreens, banana palms, ferns, and masses of flowers. Occasionally, you'll glimpse panoramic views of downtown LA and the Santa Monica Bay.

The 18½-acre park is now the property of the Beverly Hills Recreation and Parks Department.

How to Get There: From LA, go northwest on U.S. 101 to Santa Monica Blvd. and turn west. Near the 8400 block of Santa Monica Blvd., the boulevard veers sharply to the southeast (left). At this point, instead of turning, proceed straight ahead on Holloway Dr. A few blocks further on, Holloway Dr. ends at Sunset Blvd. Continue straight ahead on Sunset Blvd. A few blocks further on, Sunset Blvd. veers to the southeast (left) and Doheny Rd. goes straight ahead. Go straight ahead on Doheny Rd. to Loma Vista Dr., turn north, and proceed to the park entrance on the west (left) side of the street at 905 Loma Vista Dr. Parking on site.

The walled-in park is open daily 10–6 in summer (approximately June–September) and 10–5 the rest of the year; closed January 1, Thanksgiving, December 25, and on rainy days (the paths get slippery). The mansion is closed to the public, but some of it can be viewed from the exterior. Free; make arrangements in advance for a free guided tour, or come any time for a self-guided walk. Wear comfortable shoes, as the terrain is quite steep in places.

For Additional Information:
Beverly Hills Recreation & Parks Department
450 N. Crescent Dr.
Beverly Hills, CA 90210

213-550-4864

17. Griffith Park

Griffith Park, one of the largest municipal parks in the world, is a vast and varied natural area that clings to the slopes of the easternmost Santa Monica Mountains. In spite of the many man-made attractions that have been developed within its 4,063 acres, much of the park remains unchanged from the days when Indian villages dotted this land. The terrain edges upward from a low elevation of 384 feet to the peak of Mt. Hollywood, 1,625 feet above sea level. Tucked in among the semiarid hillsides are verdant valleys forested with oaks and sycamores and small streams edged by willows. Mule deer, fox, coyotes, bobcats, skunks, five types of snakes, and about 120 species of birds find refuge here.

Griffith Park is also the home of the 113-acre Los Angeles Zoo, which features more than 2,000 wild residents in natural settings, an animal nursery, and a petting zoo. Several koalas, the first of their subspecies to be exhibited outside of their native Australia, are displayed in a nocturnal environment. For years, the zoo's single most famous resident was Topa Topa, until recently the only California condor in captivity. He still resides here, but has been removed from public exhibit to take part in a breeding program that zoo officials hope will help save this extremely endangered species from extinction. Plants on zoo grounds, like the animals, come from around the world.

Perhaps the most famous attraction of all is Griffith Observatory and Planetarium, where you can view the lights of the city below you and the stars above you. On clear evenings, when the Observatory is open, you can peer through the twin refracting telescope free of charge. Laserium and planetarium shows are featured year-round, and exhibits in the Hall of Science depict man's relation to the universe. For descriptions of astronomical phenomena occurring in southern California skies, dial 213-663-8171 for a 24-hour recorded message.

The Ferndall Nature Museum, located near the southwest corner of the park, displays exhibits about the flora and fauna of the local area, offers guided tours, and presents a variety of educational programs. Nearby, a short nature trail skirts both sides of a spring-fed brook; a free guide available at the museum describes what you see along the way. This area, lush with ferns and exotic plants, shaded by oak and sycamore trees, is one of the most beautiful sections of the park.

Other areas and attractions of special interest include a bird sanctuary that contains a grove of redwoods and a perennial stream; the Pettigrew Science Center, where the public may view farm animals and native wildlife; one of the most complete equestrian centers in the nation, miniature train rides, Travel Town, a museum of transportation; an antique wooden carousel, pony and stagecoach rides; a Greek-style amphitheater that offers live entertainment on many summer evenings; and a visitor center than presents nature programs and movies.

Developed recreation facilities include tennis courts, golf courses, a driving range, and play areas for soccer, cricket, badminton, archery, volleyball, baseball, and softball. Scenic roads lead motorists through most sections of the park.

Hiking, Horseback Riding, and Bicycling

A 53-mile trail system takes hikers into the park's backcountry. The most popular trail runs from the parking lot of Griffith Observatory to the summit of Mt. Hollywood, a round-trip trek of 3 miles that rewards hikers with extraordinary views. Equestrians may use some of the hiking trails, as well as certain fire and patrol roads; horses may be rented by the hour at the equestrian center in the park and at stables near the park's perimeter. It's best to check at park headquarters for up-to-date information on trail closures and special restrictions before starting out; if you plan to go very far into the backcountry, advise park rangers of your intentions. Both hikers and horseback riders must be off all trails by sunset. There are short nature trails near the Ferndell Nature Museum and just south of the carousel; printed trail guides are available for each. Bicycling is allowed on all roads during park hours.

Picnicking

More than a dozen landscaped picnic areas are scattered throughout the park; facilities vary. Some have children's playgrounds nearby. No open fires are allowed anywhere in the park. Six concession stands and a full-service restaurant also lie within park boundaries.

Swimming

A public swimming pool is located in the Griffith Recreation Center near the park's southeastern corner; open 10 A.M.–noon and 1–6 P.M. during summer months. Nominal admission fee.

How to Get There: Located approximately five miles northwest of downtown LA; I-5 cuts through the easternmost border of Griffith Park, Los Feliz Blvd. lies just beyond the park's southern boundary, and CA 134 (Ventura Fwy.) runs through the northern tip of parklands. There are several park entrances. To reach the visitor center and park headquarters, located at 4730 Crystal Springs Dr. in the park's southeast quadrant, take I-5 north from downtown LA to the Griffith Park exit and follow signs.

Park open daily 5 A.M.–10:30 P.M., year-round; mountain roads close at sunset. Nominal vehicle entrance fee (less on Monday–Friday except holidays); a few facilities are located in no-fee perimeter areas outside toll booths. Additional fees charged at some attractions and recreation facilities; hours and seasons vary.

For Additional Information:
Griffith Park Visitor Center
Ranger Headquarters
4730 Crystal Springs Dr.
Los Angeles, CA 90027
213-665-5188

City of Los Angeles Department of Recreation &
    Parks
200 N. Main St., 13th Floor
Los Angeles, CA 90012
213-485-5555

Los Angeles Zoo
5333 Zoo Dr.
Los Angeles, CA 90027
213-666-4090
213-666-4650

Griffith Observatory & Planetarium
P.O. Box 27787
2800 E. Observatory Rd.
Los Angeles, CA 90027
213-664-1191 (Recording of current schedule)

Ferndell Nature Museum
Griffith Park
5375 Red Oak Dr.
Los Angeles, CA 90068
213-467-1661

18. Hancock Park

First-time visitors to southern California are invariably startled, when driving past the plethora of stores, restaurants, and hotels that lines Wilshire Boulevard west of downtown Los Angeles, to suddenly see several life-size mammoths standing near the edge of a murky pond. The pond is actually one of the world-famous La Brea Tar Pits, and the huge, elephant-like beasts are fiberglass reconstructions of animals long extinct that roamed this very land from 10,000 to 40,000 years ago.

At first glance, the pond seems ordinary enough, especially when a surface accumulation of rainwater

Mammoth at La Brea Tar Pits

camouflages the oozing tar. That's what the mammoths and other prehistoric creatures thought, too, when they waded in to get a drink and got stuck in the quagmire just beneath the film of water. The more they struggled to get out, the deeper they sank, until eventually they were completely entombed. When scientists began exploring the pits in 1905, they were delighted to find the complete and superbly preserved skeletons of such prehistoric animals as saber-toothed tigers, mastodons, ground sloths, dire wolves, short-faced bears (larger than today's Kodiak bears), and imperial mammoths (12 to 15 feet high at the shoulder). More than 100 tons of fossil bones have been removed from here thus far, making La Brea the richest source of Pleistocene epoch fossils in the world.

The Lake Pit, where the mammoth replicas stand, and several smaller pits are part of 32-acre Hancock Park. Scientists are currently excavating Pit 91, and visitors can watch the work in progress through windows at a special viewing station.

Fossils from Pit 91 are identified and catalogued at a paleontological laboratory in the George C. Page Museum, also in Hancock Park. A branch of the Los Angeles County Museum of Natural History (described elsewhere), the Page Museum displays mounted skeletons of animals recovered from the pits and a case of 404 dire wolf skulls. One of the most fascinating exhibits permits you to poke dipsticks into containers filled with La Brea tar, then try to pull them out. The extraordinary building in which the museum is housed also features an atrium garden and an imaginative gift shop. At the museum's information desk, you can pick up a free guide to all the park's features, including the sixty species of trees and shrubs found on the grounds.

Hancock Park is also the home of the Los Angeles County Museum of Art, where you'll find a cafeteria and an outdoor sculpture garden. Originally, the garden was a reflecting pool, but the pool had to be drained because of seepage from the tar pits below.

How to Get There: From downtown LA, go west on I-10 to La Brea Ave. Head north on La Brea Ave. to Wilshire Blvd., and turn west. Hancock Park lies on the north side of the 5800–5900 block of Wilshire

Blvd. between Curson Ave. on the east and Ogden Dr. on the west. Parking on site via entrance on Curson Ave. or on street.

Park open sunrise to 10 P.M. daily, year-round. Free. Scientists work at Pit 91 from 10–4 Wednesday–Sunday, year-round; closed Monday and Tuesday. Viewing station free. Page Museum open 10–5 Tuesday–Sunday, year-round; closed Monday. Nominal admission fee, free second Tuesday of each month. Scientists in museum laboratory may be observed during museum hours Wednesday–Sunday, year-round; closed Monday and Tuesday. No charge other than museum admission fee. Free guided tours of grounds at 1 P.M. Thursday–Sunday, year-round. All facilities except park grounds closed Thanksgiving, December 25, January 1.

For Additional Information:
George C. Page Museum
5801 Wilshire Blvd.
Los Angeles, CA 90036

213-936-2230
213-857-6311

19. Hollywood Reservoir

Hollywood Reservoir nestles among the foothills of the Santa Monica Mountains just west of Griffith Park (described elsewhere). Although this lovely lake lies close to the heart of the city, it is one of the least-known and most secluded spots in Los Angeles. There are no facilities—just brush-covered hillsides rising all about you, some Appian pines bordering the lake, and sweeping views of Hollywood. Occasionally, some of the wildlife in Griffith Park wanders over to the reservoir, drawn as humans are by the incredible peace of the place.

Hiking and Bicycling

Hiking and biking paths encircle the lake, a distance of 3½ miles.

How to Get There: Located northwest of LA's city center, just east of U.S. 101 (Hollywood Fwy.) and just west of Griffith Park. The reservoir is somewhat difficult to find, but well worth the effort it takes to get there. From LA, go north on U.S. 101 (Hollywood Fwy.) to Vermont Ave. Turn north on Vermont Ave. and proceed to Franklin Ave. Turn west to Beachwood Dr. Turn north to Ledgewood Dr. Turn northwest (left), and stay on Ledgewood to Mulholland Hwy. Follow the twists and turns of Mulholland to Canyon Lake Dr., and bear right. Continue on Canyon Lake to Tahoe Dr., and turn west. Proceed to Lake Hollywood Dr. at the end of Tahoe, and turn west. Lake Hollywood Dr. will head west a short way, then turn north along the eastern shore of Hollywood Reservoir. Follow the road to the north end of the reservoir. Parking on site.

Pedestrian gate open daily, year-round; 6:30–10 A.M. and 2–5 P.M. weekdays, 6:30 A.M.–5 P.M. weekends. Free.

For Additional Information:
Department of Water & Power
City of Los Angeles
111 N. Hope St.
Los Angeles, CA 90012
213-481-4211

20. Huntington Botanical Gardens

Many fine gardens are found in the greater Los Angeles area, but none surpass the beauty and superb design of these gardens in San Marino. Covering 207 acres of gently rolling hills, the grounds contain plants and trees from all parts of the plant, with something in bloom every month of the year.

The gardens began in 1904 with 10 acres of desert plants. Today, the Desert Garden covers 12 acres and contains more than 2,500 species of cacti and other succulents—the largest outdoor collection of desert plants in the world. There are other gardens, too, nearly 140 acres of them, but the improbable colors and shapes of the desert section make it the highlight of most everyone's first visit.

You'll also see ponds adorned with lilies, palm and jungle gardens, Australian and subtropical gardens, and an exquisite Japanese garden that includes a bonsai court and a walled Zen garden (one of three in the United States).

Tucked away in a special corner is a Shakespeare garden containing plants mentioned in the Bard's works. There are acres of roses and azaleas, and the 1,500 kinds of camellias found here make up the largest public collection of these flowers on earth. All together, more than 100,000 specimens representing some 10,000 species are scattered about the grounds.

Henry E. Huntington, one of the country's wealthiest businessmen in the early part of this century, purchased this land in 1902 and soon thereafter set about creating his spectacular gardens. Given Huntington's taste for the exotic in plants, it is not surprising that he was fascinated with cycads—distant relatives of the conifer that have survived from prehistoric times and are extremely rare. Of the 100 varieties that still exist throughout the world, about 50 can be seen here. Huntington also created the area's first commercial avocado grove and experimented with many other fruits as well.

Rivaling Huntington's love of plants was his love for fine art and literature. His former residence, built in 1909–1911, now houses the Huntington art collection. Nearby is the Huntington Library, noted as the greatest independent research library in the country. The rare books that fill its shelves include many works on botany.

Huntington died in 1927, but the legacy he left to the public is as beautiful as ever. Even the parking lot, dotted with avocado and eucalyptus trees and many rare herbs and plants, has been called the world's most attractive.

How to Get There: Located in Los Angeles County, northeast of LA. From LA, go northeast on CA 11 to California Blvd. and turn east to Allen Ave. Turn south and proceed on Allen until it ends at Orlando Rd. The entrance to the gardens lies on the south side of Orlando Rd., opposite the end of Allen Ave.

Open 1–4:30 Tuesday–Sunday; closed major holidays. Guided 1¼-hour tours of the gardens are normally available at 1 P.M. each Tuesday–Saturday. All free. *Note:* The City of San Marino requires Sunday visitors to have advance reservations. Tickets are free and can be ordered by mailing a self-addressed, stamped envelope to Sunday Tickets, The Huntington Library (see address below).

For Additional Information:
Huntington Botanical Gardens
1151 Oxford Rd.
San Marino, CA 91108
818-405-2100/405-2141

21. Leo Carrillo State Beach

Although this state park is most noted for its 6,600-foot beach, it has much more to offer. Most of its 1,600 acres lie inland, climbing in places to an elevation of 1,500 feet. Primarily undeveloped, the park has some heavily wooded areas of coast live oak, California sycamore, Baccharis, sumac, and willow. Mulholland Highway cuts through a rugged canyon and leads northward to the uplands of Arroyo Sequit, providing many scenic views along the way.

Roaming the isolated backcountry are coyotes, bobcats, mule deer, gray foxes, raccoons, skunks, and rattlesnakes. Bird watchers may observe hummingbirds, woodpeckers, flickers, hawks, and owls. Near the ocean shoreline, black brants, grebes, cormorants, gulls, and pelicans dart about searching for food. Sea lions and seals are occasionally spotted on offshore rocks, and from November to May, migrating gray whales can often be seen from the beach.

Carrillo's famous beach is divided into two separate areas by Sequit Point, a bluff riddled with caves and a sea-carved tunnel. At low tide, there are interesting tide pools to explore.

The park lies within the Santa Monica Mountains National Recreation Area (described elsewhere).

Hiking

A six-mile hike is possible along the Yellow Hill Fire Road, an uphill route that, on a clear day, rewards hikers with an excellent view of the Channel Islands (described elsewhere) miles out to sea. The Nicholas Flat Trail, near the entrance to Canyon Campground, climbs near sea level to 1,500-foot-high Nicholas Flat, where an ocean vista awaits you; total distance one way is 2.2 miles. A ¼-mile-long nature trail connects the north end of Canyon Campground and the group camp. Hikers also enjoy following a creek that roughly parallels Mulholland Highway.

Camping

At Beach Campground, close to the sea, are fifty family sites suitable for tents or self-contained RVs less than eight feet in height. Table and stove at each site; restroom with cold showers nearby. Canyon Campground, which parallels Mulholland Highway, has 138 family campsites for tents and RVs up to 31 feet long. Each site has table, stove, food locker, and paved parking space. Restrooms nearby; centrally located hot-shower building, park store (summers only). No hookups, but there is a sanitation dump. At the north end of Canyon Campground is a group tent camping area for up to seventy-five people; includes tables, two barbecues, restroom building with hot showers. Reservations are required for group camping; recommended in other campgrounds during summer months.

Water Sports

More than half a million visitors come to this park each year, most of them to swim, surf, and skin-dive. Each of the two beach areas has a snack bar, rest-

Leo Carillo State Park

rooms, dressing rooms, and beach equipment rental. Lifeguards are on duty year-round and can provide information about every aspect of the beach, including water conditions, hazardous areas, and the environment. Surf fishermen catch bass, perch, and cabezon.

How to Get There: Located in westernmost Los Angeles County, approximately 26 miles west of Santa Monica. From LA, go west, on I-10 to CA 1 (Pacific Coast Hwy.); take CA 1 north and then west to park, which borders both sides of the highway. Enter on north side of highway; parking on site.

Open 8–dusk daily, year-round. Nominal parking fee.

For Additional Information:
Leo Carrillo State Beach
35000 Pacific Coast Highway
Malibu, CA 90265

805-488-4111

California Department of Parks & Recreation
Santa Monica Mountains Area Headquarters
2860-A Camino Dos Rios
Newbury Park, CA 91320

818-706-1310
805-499-2112

Santa Monica Mountains National Recreation Area
22900 Ventura Blvd.
Woodland Hills, CA 91364

818-888-3770

22. Los Padres National Forest

Some of the wildest, most rugged land in California is found within the vastness of Los Padres National Forest, which straddles five mountain ranges and rambles over nearly two million acres along the state's central and southern coasts. The larger of the forest's two separate divisions extends inland from Santa Barbara and encompasses the Sierra Madre, San Rafael, Santa Ynez, and La Panza mountains, while the smaller unit further to the north embraces the Santa Lucia Mountains.

Throughout Los Padres, lofty stands of pines and firs look down upon clusters of oaks, grassy meadows, and foothills cloaked in chaparral. Red rock cliffs and great gorges slash through the forest's heart. Seven major rivers and numerous smaller streams emerge from highlands whose ocean-facing slopes receive up to 120 inches of precipitation a year, providing inexpensive water for residents of surrounding areas and recreational opportunities for the more than three million people who visit here annually.

The forest's abundance of water, diverse vegetation, and varied terrain appeal to many species of wildlife. Five—the American peregrine falcon, blunt-nosed leopard lizard, southern bald eagle, California brown pelican, and San Joaquin kit fox—are endangered. Until recently, Los Padres was also the last known nesting site for one of the rarest birds in the world. The California condor flew over the mountains and foothills of southern California for some 15,000 years, but on April 19, 1987, the last of these birds known to be living in the wild was taken into captivity about 40 miles southwest of Bakersfield, near the forest's boundary. Known officially as Adult Condor 9 (AC-9 for short) and unofficially as Igor, the nineteen-pound male was taken to the San Diego Wild Animal Park (described elsewhere), where he will reside with fourteen other California condors and participate in a breeding program scientists hope will bring the species back from the brink of extinction. These condors and thirteen more that live at the Los Angeles Zoo (described elsewhere) represent the earth's total known population of these majestic creatures. The largest land bird in North America, with wingspans up to 12 feet in width, these jet-black birds with white underwing linings have gradually succumbed to the encroachment of civilization despite one of the most ambitious programs ever initiated to save an endangered species.

One part of the effort involved setting aside two sanctuaries in Los Padres National Forest, both of which contained prime nesting sites for the reclusive birds—the 53,000-acre Sespe Condor Sanctuary, presided over by 6,210-foot-high Topatopa Peak, and the 1,200-acre Sisquoc Condor Sanctuary, deep within the San Rafael Wilderness Area. Adjoining the southern boundary of the Sespe Sanctuary is the 1,871-acre

Hopper Mountain National Wildlife Refuge, established in 1974 to preserve a feeding area favored by the condors. The refuge and both sanctuaries were closed to the general public, but an already dwindling population, hampered by a naturally low reproductive rate (a pair of condors produces one egg every other year) and possibly poisoned by lead pellets in the animal carcasses upon which they feed, continued to decline. Now, as a last resort, scientists will try a captive breeding program, hoping for a future in which the California condor will once again soar free in the wild.

Other wildlife species living in the forest include the California mule deer, Columbian black-tailed deer, bobcat, wild turkey, mountain lion, Pacific rattlesnake, wild pig, and several types of hummingbirds, hawks, bats, and sea birds. Occasionally, a black bear wanders through the woodlands. The Mount Pinos lodgepole chipmunk and Mount Pinos blue grouse live nowhere else in the world except on the mountain whose name they bear. Several species sometimes seen in the forest, such as the Barbary sheep, Rocky Mountain elk, and tahr, are escapees from the grounds of the opulent San Simeon estate built by the late William Randolph Hearst (now a state historical monument).

About one half of Los Padres—approximately that part of the larger unit that extends east and southeast of a line drawn between El Capitan State Park on the coast and the town of New Cuyama in northeastern Santa Barbara County—lies within a 100-mile radius of Los Angeles. This portion of the forest contains the tallest mountains, culminating at the 8,831-foot summit of Mount Pinos. Once visitors drove to the observation point atop this peak hoping for a glimpse of the condors who foraged in this area during summer months. Although the condors are gone, the sweeping view of the Los Padres high country, the San Joaquin Valley, and the Mojave Desert makes the trip worthwhile at any time. The scarps and sag ponds visible from the forest highway that leads west from Frazier Park to Mount Pinos mark the path.

Other attractions within our 100-mile radius include two especially scenic drives. California Highway 33 twists up and down the mountains between Ojai and Ventucopa, skirting the banks of several

creeks and the Cuyama River along the way. Just outside the forest's southern edge, you can take a short
side trip to the Black Mountain overlook near Ojai for
a far-reaching view of the Ojai Valley. This is the same
view that greeted Ronald Colman in the original
movie version of *Lost Horizon*—the enchanted valley
of Shangri-la as immortalized on film. If you come at
sunset and look beyond the valley to the northeast,
you'll see the last rays of the setting sun bathe Topatopa Peak in a rosy glow—a hushed and magical time
known locally as the "pink moment." Even the birds
stop singing.

A few miles north of Ojai, inside forest boundaries,
privately owned spas offer visitors a soak in the mineral hot springs that bubble up along Matilija Creek.

Also accessible from Highway 33 are the Piedra
Blanca area, some 600 acres of huge, uplifted white
rocks, vistas of the Cuyama Badlands, and, on clear
days, the Pacific from atop 7,500-foot-tall Pine Mountain.

Perched on the crest of the Santa Ynez Mountains
that rise behind Santa Barbara, the Camino Cielo
(Spanish for "Highway of the Sky") offers one splendid view after another. The coastal plain and sun-
dappled ocean lie far below on one side, the Santa
Ynez River and its verdant valley on the other.

Some 25 miles northeast of Santa Barbara are the
Big Caliente Hot Springs, whose waters warm to 118
degrees Fahrenheit and are piped into a concrete tank
for bathing. Located within a forest-service recreation
area, the springs are accessible via hilly and narrow
dirt roads.

Closer to Santa Barbara, but still within forest
boundaries, yet another steep road leads to the
Chumash Painted Cave, whose sandstone walls are
decorated with colorful and well-preserved Indian
artwork. Remnants of the Chumash Indian civilization are scattered throughout the forest, but many
such sites can be reached only by a lengthy trek on
foot or horseback.

Approximately half of the 143,000-acre San Rafael
Wilderness also lies within our 100-mile radius. Established in 1968, this was the first primitive area in
the nation to become a part of the National Wilderness System. Hurricane Deck, an eerie and beautiful
stretch of cliffs whose cave-pitted faces have been

contoured by the region's strong winds, is in the midst of the area.

Besides the remainder of the San Rafael Wilderness, that portion of Los Padres's larger section beyond our radius contains the 21,000-acre Santa Lucia Wilderness, bisected by picturesque Lopez Canyon, and the Cuesta Ridge Botanical Area, noted for its unusual spring wildflowers and a grove of Sargent cypress trees.

About 50 miles to the north lies the forest's second unit, well worth a visit because of its incredible beauty and unique plant life. The western border of this part of the forest edges the Pacific in places and is never far from the shoreline elsewhere. Coast-hugging California Highway 1, the only major roadway to traverse this section of Los Padres, winds along clifftops and stuns the senses with its seascapes. Along the way, numerous turnouts provide the opportunity to stop and savor what you see.

Rock hunters scour the shores of boulder-strewn Jade Cove for Monterey jade, a semiprecious, gray green stone (not to be confused with the green rocks known as pseudo jade that are also found here). Although dangerous undertows make swimming unsafe along most of the coastline adjacent to forest lands, visitors can sunbathe, picnic, explore tide pools, and hike at the water's edge in several forest-service recreation areas. Inland, they can see a tree unique to Los Padres—the rare bristlecone fir, whose entire natural range is a 60-mile-long, 12-mile-wide strip near the crest of the Santa Lucia Mountains—and the world's southernmost native stand of coast redwoods. The Ventana Wilderness, sprawled over 159,000 acres at the northern tip of the forest, contains unusual flora and outstanding geological formations.

Hiking and Horseback Riding

More than 1,750 miles of trails lead through the forest. Some were blazed by Indians and early homesteaders and have been used for centuries. One of the prettiest foothill hikes near Santa Barbara follows a 3-mile-long streamside path up Rattlesnake Canyon, passing serene pools and picturesque rock formations. Nearby, another 3-mile-long trail heads into San Ysidro Canyon, where great oaks border shallow swimming holes. The fascinating area of white rocks known as Piedra Blanca, located northeast of Ojai, is reached by a 1½-mile trail. West of Frazier Park, a 6-mile trail through coniferous forests connects Mount Pinos and Mount Abel. Longer trails penetrate the wilderness areas; free permits are required for entry. Most trails are open to both hikers and equestrians, and horse rentals are available at several stables in the vicinity.

Camping

Nearly ninety developed campgrounds are in the forest; the largest contains more than seventy sites, and several have fewer than ten sites. Fees are charged for some; others are free. Most drive-to sites accommodate both tents and trailers. Seasons and facilities vary. Virtually all have tables, stoves, and toilets, and some have drinking water; no showers, hookups, or sanitary dumps. More than 260 trailside sites with tables, stoves, and toilets are provided for backpackers.

Picnicking

Picnic areas in shady settings are situated throughout the forest. Most have tables and toilets, but only a few have drinking water. Some are located alongside swimming and fishing holes. In the northern unit, you can enjoy your picnic with an ocean view. Visitors may picnic in empty campsites, but may be charged a fee in pay campgrounds.

Water Sports

Water is the most valuable product of Los Padres. With some 485 miles of streams in the forest and thirty-five lakes and reservoirs larger than five acres on or adjacent to forest lands, opportunities abound for water sports. More than fifteen species of fish, including native and stocked trout, lure anglers to Los Padres streams. Just outside forest boundaries, the waters of lakes Cachuma, Casitas, Piru, and Pyramid teem with bass, catfish, and trout, and all four feature paved launch ramps and rental boats. The second largest largemouth bass ever caught in North America, weighing in at 21 pounds, 3¼ ounces, was pulled from Lake Casitas in 1980. Lakes Piru and Pyramid also offer swimming and waterskiing (rentals available). Within Los Padres, visitors can swim in streams near a dozen campgrounds and alongside forest roads.

Winter Sports

Winter sports facilities are available in the Mount Pinos–Mount Abel area. Toboggan runs and nearly eight miles of cross-country ski trails are open from about mid-December to mid-April. Toboggans, ski equipment, and snowshoes can be rented.

How to Get There: Located in two separate units in six counties; the larger unit, which is closer to LA and adjoins Angeles National Forest (described elsewhere) along part of its eastern border, is in Los Angeles, Ventura, Santa Barbara, Kern, and San Luis Obispo counties, while the smaller unit is in Monterey County. To reach the Mount Pinos area from LA, proceed north on I-5 through Gorman to the Frazier Mountain Park Rd. exit. Turn west and follow Frazier Mountain Park Rd. to a fork in the road at Lake of the Woods. Bear right onto Cuddy Valley Rd., and continue west, then south to Mount Pinos; look for signs. To reach other parts of the Los Padres from LA, go north, then west on U.S. 101. At Ventura, turn north onto CA 33, which leads through Ojai into the forest. Or continue through Ventura on U.S. 101 through Santa Barbara; turn north onto CA 154 and proceed into the forest. To reach the northern unit of the Los Padres in Monterey County, continue on U.S. 101 to San Luis Obispo, and turn northwest onto CA 1, which enters the forest about 20 miles north of San Simeon. Before visiting an area this size, you should obtain a forest map, which shows more than 1,600 miles of internal roads, and other literature available at any of the information sources given at the end of this listing. Ranger stations located throughout the forest can also supply information; look for signs.

Forest lands are accessible at all times. Free. Fees are charged for some facilities. Those parts of the forest that are especially susceptible to fire are closed to public access during the dry season, usually about July 1 to mid-November. Headquarters office open 8–4:45 Monday–Friday; closed some holidays. District offices generally open daily summer and fall, Monday–Friday winter and spring; hours vary; closed some holidays. Hours, days, and seasons vary for ranger stations, but they're usually open daily during heavy-use seasons.

For Additional Information:
Information Officer
Los Padres National Forest Headquarters
42 Aero Camino
Goleta, CA 93117

805-968-1578

Mount Pinos District Office
Chuchupate Ranger Station
Los Padres National Forest
Star Route, Box 400
Frazier Park, CA 93225

805-245-3731

Ojai District Office
Los Padres National Forest
1190 E. Ojai Ave.
Ojai, CA 93023

805-646-4348

Santa Barbara District Office
Los Prietos Ranger Station
Los Padres National Forest
Star Route, Paradise Rd.
Santa Barbara, CA 93105

805-967-3481

Santa Lucia District Office
Los Padres National Forest
1616 N. Carlotti Dr.
Santa Maria, CA 93454

805-925-9538

Monterey District Office
Los Padres National Forest
406 S. Mildred St.
King City, CA 93930

408-385-5434

23. MacArthur Park

At first glance, tiny MacArthur Park near downtown Los Angeles seems like any other pleasant city park, but within its 32 acres are some of the greatest varieties of trees found in any area of comparable size in all North America. Among the 107 species that grow here are the dragon palm, Bird of Paradise tree, Chinese fountain palm, California Christmas tree, pineapple guava, bald cypress, primrose tree, cutleaf weeping birch, Japanese privet, St. John's bread, southern magnolia, lemon-scented gum, strawberry tree, maiden hair tree, sausage tree, Australian fire tree, weeping bottlebrush, orchid tree, and Italian cypress. Some eighty types of trees are classified as rare. Unfortunately, at this writing, none of the trees is labeled, but the strange shapes and unusual blooms are nevertheless a botanical treat.

From October through March, the small, palm-fringed lake teems with gulls and waterfowl. Land birds seen here include Anna's hummingbird, the Chinese spotted dove, and the black Phoebe.

Picnicking

Throughout the park, picnic tables sit beneath tall shade trees.

Boating

Visitors ply the placid lake waters in rented pedal boats.

How to Get There: Located just west of downtown LA. From the intersection of U.S. 101 and CA 110, go south on CA 110 to Wilshire Blvd. and turn west. Proceed about 10 blocks to the park, which is bisected by Wilshire Blvd. The park is bordered on the east by Alvarado St., on the west by Park View St., on the north by 6th St., and on the south by 7th St.

Open from sunrise to 10 P.M. Free.

For Additional Information:
City of Los Angeles
Department of Recreation & Parks
200 N. Main St., 13th Floor
Los Angeles, CA 90012

213-485-5515

24. Malibu Creek State Park

An oasis of wild beauty, Malibu Creek State Park is primarily a walk-in park. Such natural features as rugged gorges, volcanic cliffs and buttes, grassy meadows, patches of woodland, creeks, waterfalls, rock pools, and a marshy, two-acre lake are set in a terrain that ranges from 500 to 2,200 feet above sea level. From late March throughout much of the summer, an abundance of wildflowers warm the land with vibrant color. Several huge oak trees, undisturbed for more than 500 years, exceed 20 feet in diameter. Field mice, ground squirrels, and rattlesnakes share the park with coyotes, mule deer, and an occasional mountain lion. Red-tailed hawks and golden eagles soar high above, while ducks and blue herons frequent the waterways and hummingbirds dart about in their never-ending search for food.

Prior to its acquisition by the state in 1974, this 4,000-acre area was comprised of three private properties. One part belonged to Bob Hope, another to Ronald Reagan, and the third to Twentieth Century–Fox. Perennially popular as a setting for films and television shows, the park is especially noted as the location for the "M*A*S*H" TV series.

Hiking, Horseback Riding, and Bicycling

Much of the southern part of the park is inaccessible, but its nearly vertical peaks and rocky outcroppings

MacArthur Park, Los Angeles

can often be viewed from the trail system that threads through the rest of the park. Hikers and equestrians will find about 15 miles of fire roads, trails, and undeveloped paths to follow. Some park roads are suitable for bicycling.

Fishing

Trout lurk in the waters of Malibu Creek and cattail-fringed Century Lake.

Swimming

Rock pools in Malibu Creek's gorge are favorite spots for swimming and wading.

Picnicking

An area near park headquarters has been set aside specifically for picnickers; use the entrance on the southeast corner of Mulholland Hwy. and Cornell Rd., located on the park's western edge.

How to Get There: Located in western Los Angeles County, within the boundaries of the Santa Monica Mountains National Recreation Area (described elsewhere). From LA, go north and west on U.S. 101 to Las Virgines–Malibu Canyon Rd. (Co. Hwy. N-1). Turn south and go about 4 miles (crossing over Mulholland Hwy. along the way) to the main entrance on the right side of the road. A parking area is located near the gatehouse; vehicular traffic is not permitted in most of the park.

Open 8–dusk daily, year-round. Nominal parking fee.

For Additional Information:
Malibu Creek State Park
28754 Mulholland Hwy.
Agoura, CA 91301

818-706-8809 (Monday–Friday)
818-706-1310 (Saturday and Sunday)

California Department of Parks & Recreation
Santa Monica Mountains Area Headquarters
2860-A Camino Dos Rios
Newbury Park, CA 91320

818-706-1310
805-499-2112

Santa Monica Mountains National Recreation Area
22900 Ventura Blvd.
Woodland Hills, CA 91364

818-888-3770 (Visitor information)
818-888-3440 (Headquarters)

25. Moreton Bay Fig Tree

Even in a state noted for extraordinary plant life, this tree is a standout. The gnarled giant is the largest of its species in the country and may be the largest in the northern hemisphere.

In the 1870s, the fig tree, a native of eastern Australia's Moreton Bay region, was given to a pioneer family who had a home on this site. The home is long since gone and forgotten, but the tree is now a Santa Barbara landmark, with above-ground roots that cover half a city block and a branch spread (when last measured in 1975) of 175 feet. According to the *Guinness Book of World Records,* thousands of people can stand in its shade at noon.

How to Get There: Located in the city of Santa Barbara. From LA, go north and west on U.S. 101 to State St. in Santa Barbara and turn southeast. Take State St. to Montecito St. and turn southwest. The tree is at the corner of Montecito and Chapala sts., alongside the Southern Pacific Railroad tracks and about one block southwest of the Southern Pacific Depot.

The tree is best seen during daylight hours. Free.

For Additional Information:
Conference & Visitors Ctr.
Box 299
Santa Barbara, CA 93102

805-965-3021

26. Palisades Park

Perched atop a cliff that overlooks Santa Monica State Beach, this narrow, 14-block-long strip of parkland affords superb ocean views. Visitors stroll, jog, and picnic on green velvet lawns sprinkled with flowering gardens. Gentle breezes from the sea stir palm and eucalyptus trees and cool the air on the hottest summer days. Housed in a darkened chamber in an Adult Recreation Center, the Camera Obscura captures scenes of the park and coastline in its revolving lenses, prisms, and mirrors, then projects the images in color on a circular white surface. Benches facing the ocean provide a fine place to relax, watch sea birds swoop over the water, and enjoy the sunset.

How to Get There: From LA, go west on I-10 to Ocean Ave. in Santa Monica and turn northwest. The park is hemmed in between Ocean Ave. and the edge of the cliffs. A tourist information center is located near the corner of Ocean and Arizona aves.; pick up a free walking tour brochure that points out the more than thirty species of trees found in the park. Parking on Ocean Ave. or side streets.

Park open daily, year-round, at all times. Tourist information center open daily, year-round; 10–4 in summer, 10–3 in winter. Camera Obscura open 10–4 daily (if sun shines), year-round. All free.

For Additional Information:
Department of Recreation & Parks
City of Santa Monica
2600 Ocean Park Blvd.
Santa Monica, CA 90405
213-458-8311

Convention & Visitors Bureau
Box 5278
Santa Monica, CA 90405
213-372-9631

Visitors Center
Palisades Park
213-343-7593

27. Park Memorial Garden

A place of serene beauty in the midst of Santa Barbara, this 4½-acre garden offers a diversity of local plant life in environments that range from marshy to arid. Some 300 varieties of flowers, trees, shrubs, and ground covers are found here, providing an array of colors every season of the year. A small pond hosts several types of marine plants, and two streams meander through the grounds. Benches placed along winding pathways invite visitors to relax.

Developed on land given to the city by Alice Keck Park, the garden is designed in accordance with her wishes. It adjoins Alameda Plaza (described elsewhere).

How to Get There: From LA, drive north on U.S. 101 to Santa Barbara. At the Carillo St. exit, take Carillo St. northwest to Santa Barbara St. and turn northwest (left). The garden is located on the northeast (right) side of Santa Barbara St., just after you pass Alameda Plaza. Parking on street.

Open daily at all times. Free.

For Additional Information:
Parks Director
City of Santa Barbara
620 Laguna St.
Santa Barbara, CA 93102

805-963-0611

28. Pico Oak

An oddity of nature, the Pico Oak grows in an open field in the Santa Clarita Valley. Its base forms a large arch, with the main trunk towering up from the center of the arc.

Although the oak stands behind a fence on private property, you can easily view it—in all its twisted, sprawling splendor—from the road.

Pico Oak is sometimes referred to as the Ripley Oak, because it was featured in Ripley's "Believe It or Not" newspaper column and also in one of Ripley's books.

How to Get There: Located in northwestern Los Angeles County near Newhall. From LA, take I-5 north to the Lyons Ave.–Pico Canyon off ramp. Exit, turn west onto Pico Canyon Rd., proceed a short distance, and look for Pico Oak on the left side of the road. It stands—quite alone—approximately ⅓ mile west of I-5 and about 75 feet south of Pico Canyon Rd.

For Additional Information:
Newhall Chamber of Commerce
23920 Valencia Blvd., #125
Valencia, CA 91355

805-259-4787

29. Placerita Canyon State and County Park

This 350-acre park is best known as the place where the California gold rush began. Francisco Lopez, while herding cattle with two companions on March 9, 1842, paused to take a nap under an oak tree. Upon awakening, he dug up a nearby cluster of wild onions with which to spice up his lunch. When he noticed the glistening yellow particles clinging to the dark skin of his hand, lunch was forgotten. Francisco collected more particles and rushed off to the Los Angeles assay office, where he learned that his find was indeed placer gold. The news of his discovery started an epidemic of gold fever seven years before the more famous gold rush in northern California.

Today, the tree that once shaded Lopez is a state historical monument known as the "Oak of the Golden Dream." It grows—weathered and gnarled—beside a bubbling brook near the park entrance.

The cool green valley surrounding it is studded with sycamores, cottonwoods, and many oaks. Most of the gold is gone, but in the spring and summer, golden wildflowers grow in abundance. Much of the land is wild, climbing from the canyon floor to the crest of the San Gabriel Mountains, where it meets the Angeles National Forest (described elsewhere).

Because of the diversified terrain, a variety of flora and fauna thrive here. Bird and plant checklists are available in the park.

Although the park is owned by the state of California, it is administered by the County of Los Angeles, and the nature center is one of the finest in the Los Angeles County park system.

Hiking and Horseback Riding

Approximately 8 miles of trails are located in the park. The 7-mile-long Los Pinetos Trail for hikers and equestrians lies partly in the adjoining Angeles National Forest. Other trails that lie entirely within the park—some easy, some rigorous—lead to such points of interest as a breathtaking waterfall, the Oak of the Golden Dream, and a restored cabin (circa 1920) used in the filming of movies and early television shows. Two self-guiding nature trails begin near the nature center, where trail guides are available.

Picnicking

An inviting picnic area along Placerita Creek offers seventy-five tables and numerous wood-burning stoves. Playground equipment is nearby.

How to Get There: Located in northwestern Los Angeles County. From LA, take I-5 north to CA 14 (Antelope Valley Fwy.). Go northeast on CA 14 to Placerita Canyon Rd. and turn east. Proceed about 2 miles to the park entrance on the south (right) side of the road.

   Park gates and nature center open 9–5 daily; closed December 25. Free.

For Additional Information:
Placerita Canyon Nature Center
19152 W. Placerita Canyon Rd.
Newhall, CA 91321
805-259-7721

County of Los Angeles
Department of Parks & Recreation
433 S. Vermont Ave.
Los Angeles, CA 90020
213-738-2961

30. Plaza Park

Plaza Park covers just one square block in the heart of downtown Ventura, but its wide expanse of green lawn, colorful flower beds, and huge, graceful old trees make it well worth seeing. Particularly notable is the Moreton Bay fig tree that stands in the park's northwest corner. The largest tree in Ventura, it's 68 feet tall and has a branch spread of 130 feet, a root spread of 81 feet, and a circumference, at 5 feet above the ground, of 21 feet, 8 inches. A plaque beneath the tree discloses that it was planted in 1874.

Picnicking

Several picnic tables rest on the shaded lawn; restrooms, drinking water, and playground equipment are provided.

How to Get There: From LA, go northwest on U.S. 101 to Ventura. Take the California St. off ramp and turn north. Almost immediately, you will reach the intersection of California and Thompson Blvd. Turn east onto Thompson, and proceed one block to the intersection of Thompson and S. Chestnut St. Plaza Park extends northeast from this intersection; it's bounded by Thompson on the south, Chestnut on the west, Santa Clara St. on the north, and Fir St. on the east.

   Open at all times. Free.

For Additional Information:
Ventura Parks & Recreation Dept.
Box 99
Ventura, CA 93002

805-654-7800

Ventura Visitor & Convention Bureau
785 S. Seaward Ave., Suite B
Ventura, CA 93001

805-648-2075 or
(within CA) 800-443-0100

31. Point Mugu State Park

One of southern California's most varied state parks is Point Mugu, 13,000 acres of canyons, mountains, ocean shoreline, and broad grassy meadows dotted with sycamores, oaks, and a few native walnuts. Inland springs surrounded by gardens of ferns are not far from the desert atmosphere of chaparral-covered hillsides. Several small streams tumble down mountainsides and make their way to a shoreline edged with rocky bluffs, sandy beaches, and a spectacular sand dune.

   In the heart of the park, accessible only on foot or

on horseback, are two fine natural areas. La Jolla Valley is a remnant of native tall-grass prairie where wildflowers bloom in abundance each spring; Big Sycamore Canyon contains riparian woodlands and the finest example of a sycamore savannah in the state park system. It is also a wintering area for monarch butterflies.

Located at the western edge of the Santa Monica Mountains National Recreation Area (described elsewhere), these parklands are rich in wildlife most of the year. Bobcats, striped and spotted skunks, mountain lions, badgers, and gray foxes live here but are seldom seen. Ground squirrels, mule deer, seals, and sea lions are more frequently sighted. During the winter and early spring, visitors may spot gray whales on their annual migration between Baja and Alaska.

Raptors, owls, and red-winged blackbirds nest in the park. Just outside the park's southwest corner lies Mugu Lagoon, the largest coastal wetland in southern California. Nearly 200 species of birds have been sighted here, and approximately 10,000 birds make this their winter home. Many of them, including the endangered brown pelican and California least tern, also visit Point Mugu State Park.

Although the lagoon is within the boundaries of the U.S. Navy Pacific Missile Test Center and therefore off-limits to the general public, it can be observed from an overlook located on CA 1 about ½ mile north of Point Mugu Rock. The navy also conducts group interpretive tours for fifteen to twenty-five adults on weekends. Reservations are necessary and may be made by calling the center's Public Affairs Office at 805-982-8094.

Hiking, Horseback Riding, and Bicycling

More than 70 miles of trails for hiking and horseback riding traverse the park; many are dual-purpose, while some are for hikers only. Some trails are also appropriate for bicycling. One of the three major trails leads into Big Sycamore Canyon, another through La Jolla Valley, while a third follows the divide between the other two. The latter, known as the Overlook Trail, affords breathtaking vistas that include occasional views of the ocean and the Channel Islands (described elsewhere). Several connecting trails, shortcuts, and loop trails meet the major trails. Interpretive hikes are led by park naturalists during the summer.

Camping

Three campgrounds are located within the park. Sycamore Canyon Campground with 55 sites and La Jolla Beach Campground with 102 sites, both along CA 1, offer primitive camping for tents and trailers up to 31 feet. No hookups; piped drinking water, chemical toilets, tables, and stoves. A trailer sanitation station is provided at La Jolla Beach. Reservations may be made for either at Ticketron outlets or by mail from Ticketron, P.O. Box 26430, San Francisco, CA 94126. A primitive walk-in campground at La Jolla Valley, two miles from the nearest access point, is available on a first-come-first-served basis, but you must register at an entrance station or park headquarters at least an hour before sunset; twelve family sites, group camping area with twenty-five sites, tables, drinking water, restrooms. All campgrounds open year-round, except during periods of extreme fire danger; very crowded mid-June through September.

Picnicking

A picnic area with tables and charcoal-burning stoves is located at Sycamore Cove, just off CA 1, near park headquarters.

Water Sports

Swimming, surf fishing, skin diving, body surfing, and beachcombing are all popular activities along the park's 5 miles of ocean shoreline. Lifeguards are on duty during the summer months; you're advised to swim only in a guarded area.

How to Get There: Located along the Pacific coast in southeastern Ventura County. From LA, go west on I-10 to CA 1 (Pacific Coast Hwy.); take CA 1 north and then west to park, which borders both sides of the highway. Park headquarters are at Sycamore Cove Beach on the south side of CA 1; parking on site.

Open 8–dusk daily, year-round. Nominal parking fee.

For Additional Information:
Point Mugu State Park
9000 West Pacific Coast Hwy.
Malibu, CA 90265

818-706-1310
818-987-3303

California Department of Parks & Recreation
Santa Monica Mountains Area Headquarters
2860-A Camino Dos Rios
Newbury Park, CA 91320

818-706-1310
805-499-2112

Santa Monica Mountains National Recreation Area
22900 Ventura Blvd.
Woodland Hills, CA 91364

818-888-3770

32. Robinson Gardens

Only recently opened to the public, the exquisite Virginia Robinson Gardens cover more than 6 hillside acres. The creation of the patio gardens began in 1911 when Mrs. Robinson and her husband, Harry Winchester Robinson, moved into the home they had built on these grounds.

At the time, only an elderberry bush grew on the property. Today, there are roses, camellias, orchids, azaleas, many unusual trees now more than sixty years old, and a unique palm grove, as well as many other flowers, shrubs, and fruit trees. Interlocking footpaths and brick stairways provide access to every part of the grounds.

Mrs. Robinson, who survived her husband and lived here until her death in 1977 at age ninety-nine, willed the entire property to the County of Los Angeles to be maintained as a public botanic garden. Listed on the National Register of Historic Places, the Robinson estate was one of the first and finest residences built in Beverly Hills.

How to Get There: Located in Beverly Hills, near the intersection of I-405 and Ventura Blvd.

At present, the gardens are open by appointment only. Guided walking tours that last approximately 1½ hours begin at 10 A.M. and 1 P.M. each Tuesday–Friday. Comfortable walking shoes are recommended. Exact directions will be given when you make your reservations; limited parking on site. If possible, phone at least one month prior to your visit. Admission is charged; group tours limited to thirty people.

For Additional Information:
Los Angeles State & County Arboretum
Attn: Robinson Gardens
301 N. Baldwin Ave.
Arcadia, CA 91006

818-446-8251

33. Santa Barbara Botanic Garden

An excellent place to study California's great variety of native plant life is the 65-acre Santa Barbara Botanic Garden, located in a beautiful setting that includes a canyon floor, chaparral-covered slopes, Mission Creek, and a view of the Santa Ynez Mountains to the north. Spring is the most colorful season, but the garden, divided into several geographical sections, is interesting at any time of the year.

Of particular note are the Ceanothus section, which blankets the landscape with blue and white blooms and fills the air with sweetness from February through April; the meadow section, with its giant oaks, borders of flowering shrubs, and an attractive water garden; the redwood section, whose tall, impressive trees were planted in the 1920s during the garden's early days; the desert section, bright with blooms in early summer; and the island section, devoted to the unusual flora of California's sea islands.

Wear comfortable walking shoes; there are 5 miles of trails, and some are steep in places.

Also on the grounds are a gift and book shop, a botanical library, and a research herbarium. The garden occasionally sponsors naturalist-guided tours to other parts of California and the West.

How to Get There: From LA, drive north on U.S. 101 to Santa Barbara. Exit at Mission St., proceed northeast to Mission Canyon Rd., turn north and go to the garden, which borders both sides of the road. (Along the way, at Foothill Rd., Mission Canyon Rd. cuts to the right.) Parking and main entrance are on the west side of Mission Canyon Rd.

Garden open 8–sunset daily; guided tours at 10:30 Thursday. Free admission; maps and trail guides available for nominal fee. Shop open 10–4 Monday–Saturday, 11–4 Sunday.

For Additional Information:
Santa Barbara Botanic Garden
1212 Mission Canyon Rd.
Santa Barbara, CA 93105

805-682-4726

34. Santa Barbara Museum of Natural History

A few years ago, a giant whale washed up on a Santa Barbara beach. Today, its 70-foot skeleton has been assembled next to the parking lot of the Santa Barbara Museum of Natural History as one of the museum's newest exhibits. The whale fits nicely into the museum's focus on the natural history of southern and central coastal California and the offshore Channel Islands.

Another particularly notable display is a stuffed specimen of the critically endangered California condor, whose last living relatives made their final stand in the wild in nearby Los Padres National Forest. The condor population is currently estimated at fewer than twenty-five birds, all in captivity.

When it was founded in 1916, the museum was limited to collections and research in the field of ornithology. That heritage is apparent in the nearly 500 stuffed birds, some 3,200 bird skins, and 4,500 sets of eggs now housed in the museum.

In 1923, the institution's scope was broadened to include all aspects of natural history, and visitors will also see exhibits on animals, plants, minerals, gems, marine life, and geology.

In addition to the exhibition halls, the museum contains a planetarium, observatory, reference library, and gift shop. Special programs such as local field trips, whale-watching excursions, Channel Island tours, and nature walks are offered throughout the year.

How to Get There: From LA, drive north on U.S. 101 to Santa Barbara, take Mission St. northeast to Mission Canyon Rd., and turn north (right). Proceed to the museum sign on the west side of Mission Canyon Rd., turn west (left) onto Puesta del Sol Rd., and continue a short distance to the museum.

Open 9–5 Monday–Saturday, 10–5 summer Sundays and holidays, 1–5 Sundays and holidays rest of year; closed Thanksgiving, December 25. Free admission; free guided tours at 2 each Sunday. Admission fee for planetarium; phone for schedule.

For Additional Information:
Santa Barbara Museum of Natural History
2559 Puesta del Sol Rd.
Santa Barbara, CA 93105

805-682-4711 (General information)
805-682-4334
805-682-3224

35. Santa Barbara Orchid Estate

Any month of the year, you can see more than 100 varieties of orchids in bloom at the Santa Barbara Orchid Estate. Some of the blossoms are so tiny they can only be effectively seen under a magnifying glass.

Located on two acres—one outdoors, one under glass—the estate is irresistible to admirers of these delicate flowers. This is a commercial enterprise, but visitors are always welcome to stroll among the plants and enjoy their beauty. Both cut flowers and plants are on sale, and an annual orchid fair is held here during the third weekend of July.

How to Get There: From LA, drive north on U.S. 101 through Santa Barbara to the small community of Goleta. At the Patterson Ave. exit, turn south and follow Patterson until it ends at Shoreline Dr. Go east on

Shoreline to Orchid Dr. and turn south. The gardens are located at 1250 Orchid Dr.

Open 9–5 daily.

For Additional Information:
Santa Barbara Orchid Estate
1250 Orchid Dr.
Santa Barbara, CA 93111

805-967-1284

36. Santa Barbara Zoological Gardens

This small but charming zoo, also known as A Child's Estate, is specifically designed for children. All animals can be seen from a pint-size viewpoint.

Animals include bears, elephants, tigers, lions, pumas, llamas, and the desert tortoise (California's official reptile). One of the most popular exhibits is a sealarium with see-through portholes for underwater viewing. In a farmyard petting area, children sometimes chase the animals and animals sometimes chase the children; pygmy goat kids may be purchased.

What looks like a tangle of many snakes in the Reptile House is actually two mammoth pythons. On an island in a lagoon, Gibbon apes delight onlookers with their acrobatic play. The lagoon is part of the adjacent Andrée Clark Bird Refuge (described elsewhere).

A miniature railroad offers rides around the grounds.

Picnicking

Several picnic tables atop a grassy hill offer an impressive view of Santa Barbara Harbor. In a nearby playground, children can climb rocks, crawl through tunnels, and explore a pirate ship and covered wagon. A concession stand sells snacks.

How to Get There: From LA, take U.S. 101 northwest to Santa Barbara and exit west onto Cabrillo Blvd. Go to Ninos Dr., turn north, and proceed to the zoo on the east side of the road. Look for signs.

Open 10–5 daily; closed Thanksgiving, December

25, and Fiesta Parade Day (early August). Entrance fee; under 2 free.

For Additional Information:
Santa Barbara Zoological Gardens
500 Ninos Dr.
Santa Barbara, CA 93103
805-962-6310

37. Santa Monica Mountains National Recreation Area

The rugged Santa Monica Mountains provide a wilderness playground that lies within an hour's drive of some 10 million people. From their eastern terminus in Griffith Park (a Los Angeles city park described elsewhere), the mountains march westward for 50 miles, climbing to an elevation of more than 3,000 feet before plunging into the sea at Point Mugu State Park.

Approximately 150,000 of the 240,000 acres that make up the mountain ecosystem lie within the boundaries of the Santa Monica Mountains National Recreation Area, added to the national park system in 1978. The cooperative management concept used here, a first for the National Park Service, permits a majority of the NRA to remain in private ownership. State and local parklands continue to be managed by their respective administrative agencies, while the National Park Service concentrates on gradually acquiring land that will enhance existing recreational facilities and preserve notable natural and historic features.

The entire NRA is a place of wondrous ecological diversity. Inland, canyons etched deep into the mountains are passageways for small streams rushing to join the waters of the Pacific. Some of the complex geology of the area, created by faulting, folding, and volcanism, may be read on canyon walls. Scattered throughout the mountains are placid pools of water, seasonal waterfalls, freshwater springs, native prairie grasslands, oak and sycamore forests, fern glens, and a type of chaparral community that is found on this continent only in southern California.

Along the NRA's southern boundary are nearly 50

miles of breathtaking coastline, still relatively undisturbed despite the fact that it receives some of the most intense recreational use in the country. The waters of the Pacific lap at long white beaches interspersed with rock outcroppings and high bluffs riddled with small caves, then temporarily withdraw to reveal tide pools teeming with life.

Mountain lions and bobcats roam wild in the mountains, along with an abundance of deer and coyotes. Hawks maneuver through the air, and golden eagles nest in mountain cliffs overlooking streams that shelter spawning steelhead trout. In spring and fall, the massive numbers of birds that migrate along the Pacific Flyway pause to rest on coastal lagoons and marshes. California sea lions and harbor seals may occasionally be seen on offshore rocks.

Plant life, nurtured by southern California's Mediterranean climate, is as diverse as the wildlife and thrives year-round. Visually, however, it is most spectacular in early spring, when myriads of wildflowers bloom brightly on fresh green meadows and the plants of the chaparral put forth their showiest blossoms.

Perhaps the most famous of the park's many scenic roads is Mulholland Drive and Highway (Drive within LA city limits, Highway when it leaves them). Lying entirely inside NRA boundaries, the low-speed road twists along the crest of the Santa Monica Mountains for approximately 50 miles and affords spectacular views all along the way. For close-up vistas of the ocean, follow CA 1 (Pacific Coast Highway), which hugs the shoreline from one end of the NRA to the other.

Several of the parklands in the NRA—Topanga, Malibu Creek, and Point Mugu state parks, Leo Carrillo State Beach, Will Rogers State Historic Park, Charmlee and Tapia county parks, and Cold Creek Canyon Preserve—are described elsewhere in more detail. Some of the other sites open to the public are:

Castro Crest

Wild backcountry; one of the most isolated areas currently open to the public. Good place to study the relationship of local flora to the fires that often sweep the chaparral-covered slopes of the Santa Monica Mountains.

Cheeseboro Canyon

Outstanding natural area. Golden eagles, falcons, and hawks live in abundance on this 1,700-acre site. Undulating grasslands dotted with huge 400-year-old oaks border a year-round stream. Ranger-led hikes on weekends.

Coldwater Canyon Park

Headquarters for the Tree People, a nonprofit organization dedicated to planting smog-resistant trees in southern California areas damaged by air pollution. Slide shows on trees, urban forestry, smog, and solar energy; nature trails, tree nurseries, gardens.

Franklin Canyon Ranch

Explore a cool canyon and the oldest rocks in the Santa Monica Mountains. Views of western Los Angeles from the mountaintops. Many free educational programs for families and groups of all ages; nature hikes and jogs, flora and fauna identification walks, nature photography, sensory hikes, evening hikes that include stargazing through a telescope, slide shows.

Malibu Lagoon State Beach

More than 200 species of birds, including the endangered light-footed clapper rail, have been observed at the recently restored lagoon. Fed by Malibu Creek, one of the few watercourses in southern California where steelhead trout spawn, the lagoon is a resting place for the migrant birds that travel the Pacific Flyway.

Paramount Ranch

336 acres of pastoral meadows and gentle hills, formerly owned by Paramount Studios. On weekends, rangers lead hikes and conduct tours of a western town set still used by television and movie companies. Two annual events are held here—the Renais-

sance Pleasure Faire in late spring and the Santa
Monica Mountains Folklife Festival in June.

Point Dume State Beach

Also known as Westward Beach. Sand pocket
beaches, rocky shores, reefs and kelp beds offshore,
many small caves, 200-foot-high bluffs, 35-acre ecological reserve. Two plant species endemic to California—the giant coreopsis and the live-forever—reach
their southern limit here. The endangered California
brown pelican can sometimes be spotted perching on
offshore rocks. Near the west end of the beach, a stairway leads up to the Point Dume Whale Watch, a fine
place to see migrating California gray whales from
mid-December to late March and to view a Pacific
panorama at any time.

Rancho Sierra Vista

Large, grassy fields and chaparral-covered hillsides
provide the setting for a Native American cultural
center, now under development. Ranger-led hikes
available on reservation basis. The National Park Service hopes to also use this area for outdoor education
programs and as the locale of a living history farm.

Rocky Oaks Ranch

Oak groves, small pond, plant communities of chaparral and coastal sagebrush, and views of rock formations created 10 to 15 million years ago by volcanic
eruption. Guided hikes on weekends.

Strauss Ranch

Restored gardens. Cultural events held in amphitheater and ranch house.

Many more lands in the NRA are open to the public
at this writing, and new units are being acquired as
budget permits. For up-to-date information about the
status of the NRA, as well as schedules of special
programs and events, write, phone, or visit the information center located in the National Park Service
headquarters building in Woodland Hills.

Hiking, Horseback Riding, and Bicycling

Many miles of hiking, equestrian, and bicycling trails already exist within the NRA, and many more are planned. Horses and bicycles may be rented at several places in and near the NRA. At present, equestrians are permitted on nearly all trails and fire roads on public lands except those on state beaches. Bicyclists are allowed to ride in certain areas of most state parks, and there are established bike paths at Tapia County Park and Santa Monica State Beach. The Pacific Coast Bicentennial Route, a 1,000-mile-long bike path that follows the coast as closely as possible from the California-Oregon border to Mexico, passes through the NRA. A 55-mile-long hiking trail that will follow the backbone of the Santa Monica Mountains from Will Rogers State Historic Park on the east to Point Mugu State Park on the west is currently being established; portions of the trail are already open. Guided hikes are offered on a regular basis throughout the NRA; schedule available at the Visitor Information Center.

Camping

Family campgrounds that accommodate both RVs and tents are currently available at Point Mugu State Park and Leo Carrillo State Beach (both described elsewhere). Group camping, walk-in tent camping, and equestrian camping are offered on a limited basis in other parts of the NRA.

Picnicking

Picnic areas abound throughout the NRA. Some offer an ocean view, others are nestled in cool canyons, still others are in shaded bowers on the banks of small streams. Many are secluded, while others are near major recreation facilities.

Water Sports

Much of the NRA's coastline is in public ownership, and the beaches—some operated by the state, some by Los Angeles County—are among the finest in southern California. Those at Point Mugu State Park and Leo Carrillo State Beach (both described elsewhere) lie near the western end of the recreation area. Between them and the city of Santa Monica are nearly fifteen more public beaches, each with its own distinct personality.

Among the best swimming beaches are those at Nicholas Canyon County Beach, Malibu Lagoon and Will Rogers state beaches, Zuma Beach County Park, and Point Dume State Park. The finest surfing is found at world-famous Surfrider State Beach (adjacent to Malibu Lagoon State Beach); surfing is also popular at Leo Carrillo, Topanga, and Santa Monica state beaches and at County Line Beach, about 1½ miles west of the Ventura–Los Angeles county line. Favorite spots for skin and scuba divers who want to explore offshore reefs and kelp beds include Point Mugu State Park, Leo Carrillo, Malibu Lagoon, Corral (also known as Solstice), and Las Tunas state beaches, Zuma Beach County Park, and Paradise Cove, a privately owned beach open to the public. Point Dume State Beach, with its swift currents and rapid drop-off in depth, lures more experienced divers. Rental equipment is available at several commercial establishments in the area.

Surf fishing, permitted at most public beaches, produces catches of barred and walleye perch, spotfin and yellowfin croakers, corbina, and an occasional halibut. Grunion (described elsewhere) come ashore on all beaches in the NRA and may be collected by hand in March, June, July, and August. Fishing piers, rental boats, licenses, and bait and tackle are available at Malibu, Santa Monica, and Paradise Cove (near Point Dume State Beach); charter boats at Santa Monica and Paradise Cove carry fishermen far offshore for such deep-sea catches as silver salmon (spring to summer), barracuda, bonito, halibut, kelp bass, mackerel, rockfish, and sheephead.

How to Get There: Located in western Los Angeles County and southeastern Ventura County. The NRA's southern boundary is formed by the Pacific Ocean; the westernmost boundary lies not far west of Point Mugu State Park; the easternmost point is at the intersection of U.S. 101 (Hollywood Fwy.) and Mulholland Dr.; the northernmost point of land is in Cheeseboro Canyon, which runs north from Ventura Fwy. near Agoura. The NRA's two major roads run generally east and west. To reach the first, CA 1 (Pacific Coast Hwy.), go west from LA on I-10, which meets CA 1 in Santa Monica. Follow CA 1 west along the Pacific shoreline. To reach the second, Mulholland Dr. and Hwy., go north from LA on U.S. 101 (Hollywood

Fwy.) to Hollywood. Turn west on Mulholland and proceed to Leo Carrillo State Beach, where the road veers south through the park and joins CA 1 near the ocean. One 10-mile stretch of Mulholland, west from I-405 to Topanga Canyon Blvd., is unpaved at this writing. Throughout the NRA, many north/south roads provide connecting routes between Mulholland and CA 1.

Most publicly owned NRA units are open daily, year-round, except during times of high fire danger; hours vary. Some are free; some charge nominal parking fees. For exact directions to a specific unit, contact the National Park Service information center.

For Additional Information:
Santa Monica Mountains National Recreation Area
22900 Ventura Blvd.
Woodland Hills, CA 91364

818-888-3770 (Visitor information)
818-888-3440 (Headquarters)

California Department of Parks & Recreation
Santa Monica Mountains Area Headquarters
2860-A Camino Dos Rios
Newbury Park, CA 91320

818-706-1310

County of Los Angeles
Department of Parks & Recreation
433 S. Vermont Ave.
Los Angeles, CA 90020

213-738-2961

The Tree People
12601 Mulholland Dr.
Beverly Hills, CA 90210
818-769-2663

38. Self-Realization Fellowship Lake Shrine

This serene sanctuary nestled in a small ravine was created by the Self-Realization Fellowship, a religious sect that believes in the universality of all religions and the glorification of flora. Paramahansa Yogananda, the Indian mystic who founded the Fellowship, purchased this 10-acre site in 1950 and transformed it into his own vision of paradise, to be shared with any and all visitors.

Patches of emerald lawns merge with dense growths of luxuriant foliage. Most of the year, the landscape is bright with blossoms. A pathway skirts the shore of a small, spring-fed lake that's home to an assortment of ducks and swans. Throughout the grounds, there are secluded spots in which to pause and meditate.

An authentic replica of a Dutch windmill contains the Fellowship's chapel. Just behind the Golden Lotus Archway, a series of white posts and beams topped with golden domes, is a sarcophagus that holds a portion of Mahatma Gandhi's ashes.

How to Get There: Located in western Los Angeles County. From LA, go west on I-10 to CA 1 (Pacific Coast Hwy.). Go north and west on CA 1 to Sunset Blvd. in Pacific Palisades. Turn north on Sunset Blvd. and proceed approximately ½ mile to the Lake Shrine entrance on the right side of the road at 17190 Sunset Blvd. Parking on site.

Open 9–5 Tuesday–Sunday; closed Monday. Free.

For Additional Information:
Self-Realization Fellowship Lake Shrine
17190 Sunset Blvd.
Pacific Palisades, CA 90272

213-454-4114

39. Sequoia National Forest

Sequoia National Forest sprawls over the southern end of the Sierra Nevada Mountains and provides some of the most spectacular views of rugged mountain landscape in the entire West. Within its boundaries are peaks more than 12,000 feet high, mountain meadows, picturesque granite domes and rock outcroppings, singing streams, placid high-country lakes, natural hot springs, precipitous canyons, tumbling waterfalls, and some thirty groves of the massive trees for which the forest is named.

One sequoia 269 feet high and 90 feet in circumference is the largest tree to be found in the national forests of the United States and the third largest of its species anywhere. Known as the Boole Tree, this giant is located in Converse Mountain Grove in the northernmost part of the forest. Not far to the southwest, a trail leads to the Chicago Stump, all that remains of what may have been the largest sequoia ever grown. The tree was felled in 1893, cut into pieces, shipped to Chicago, and reassembled for display at the World's Columbian Exposition. Astonished visitors, who didn't believe a tree could be so big, declared it a hoax.

The forest borders the Inyo and Sierra national forests, as well as the Kings Canyon and Sequoia national parks, and is part of a virtually unbroken green belt of federally owned land that extends northward from near Bakersfield to the Oregon border. Only a few thousand of the 1,180,000 acres contained within Sequoia National Forest's four separate units lie within the 100-mile radius set for this book, but they offer an experience unique in southern California—whitewater rafting.

Here the Kern River surges through a narrow, boulder-strewn canyon on the final leg of its 165-mile journey from high Sierras to desert lowlands. In places, the river flows serenely. Verdant growths of willow, cottonwood, and maple, lush as a jungle, crowd the shorelines. The air is filled with birdsong, turtles sun themselves on logs and rocks that dot the waterway, and lazing bullfrogs can be caught with bare hands. In other places, the churning waters create Class III, IV, and V rapids that take your breath away. The Kern, one of the swiftest and steepest rivers on the continent, boasts a gradient of 30 feet or more per mile.

Several commercial outfitters, regulated by the U.S. Forest Service, offer guided, half-day- to two-day-long raft trips on the Lower Kern from May into October. For a list of their names, contact one of the information sources given at the end of this entry. Experienced do-it-yourselfers may also run the river in rafts or kayaks (canoes are not recommended) if they obtain permits in advance.

Landlubbers can view much of the canyon's wild beauty from CA 178, a scenic highway that parallels this section of the river.

Except for the Lower Kern, which flows westward,

the river follows a north-to-south route and provides additional whitewater runs. One 18-mile segment known as the Forks of the Kern, which drops 60 feet per mile, may be the finest stretch of raftable whitewater in North America. Most outfitters who guide trips on the Lower Kern also offer trips on other portions of the river.

Although the Kern River is the forest's most popular attraction, there are hundreds of miles of forest roads to explore and hundreds of thousands of acres of wilderness where visitors on foot and horseback travel in the company of eagles. Autumn brings stunning fall color to parts of the forest, and winter, when the snow pack is deep enough, lures cross-country skiers.

Hiking and Horseback Riding

More than 1,300 miles of hiking and riding trails traverse all parts of the forest, including nearly 80 miles of the Pacific Crest National Scenic Trail (described elsewhere). The 3-mile-long Jackass Creek Trail and 12-mile-long Summit Trail have been designated national recreation trails. Since the forest ranges in elevation from 1,000 to 12,000 feet, hiking can be as rugged as you like.

Several commercial facilities near forest boundaries rent horses and equipment for backcountry pack trips or day rides. Ranger stations can provide a current list of stables and packers.

Fishing

Fishing is permitted in nearly all forest waters, but the Kern River is the most popular place to wet a line. Anglers try for rainbow trout in the rapids and bass in stillwater pools.

Camping

Some sixty forest campgrounds contain about 1,200 family campsites in attractive settings. A few are located adjacent to sequoia groves; some are on the banks of the Kern River. Facilities, fees, and seasons vary; primitive sites are free. No hookups. A few forest sites, open from spring through fall, are located along CA 178 in the Lower Kern River Canyon. Further east along CA 178, about 3 miles beyond the forest boundary, lies Isabella Lake, a man-made lake backed up behind a dam on the Kern River. It's managed by the U.S. Army Corps of Engineers, which has established several campgrounds along its shore. Additional campgrounds within or near forest boundaries, some with hookups, are operated by private owners and local public agencies.

Picnicking

Several picnic areas in a variety of scenic settings are found along forest roads. All have tables; some have drinking water and toilets. Bank fishing is a special feature at some streamside locations.

How to Get There: Sequoia National Forest is located, from south to north, in Kern, Tulare, and Fresno counties. The portion of the Lower Kern River, its canyon, and surrounding woodlands found within the 100-mile radius prescribed for this book lie in northeastern Kern County in the forest's Greenhorn Ranger District. From LA, take I-5 north to its junction with CA 99, then continue north on CA 99 to Bakersfield. Turn east onto CA 178 and proceed about 20 miles to the southwestern boundary of the forest. Visitors can obtain information and, for a nominal fee, purchase a map of Sequoia National Forest at the headquarters office or any one of five district ranger stations.

Forest lands accessible at all times. Free. Headquarters office and Greenhorn Ranger District (the ranger station closest to LA) open 8–4:30 Monday–Friday; closed some holidays. Ranger stations further to the north are open daily in the summer, Monday–Friday in the winter; hours vary.

For Additional Information:
Information Officer
Sequoia National Forest Headquarters
900 W. Grand Ave.
Porterville, CA 93257

209-784-1500

Greenhorn Ranger District
Sequoia National Forest
800 Truxtun Ave.
Room 322, Federal Bldg.
Bakersfield, CA 93301

805-861-4212

40. Steckel Park

Steckel Park, covering 138 acres near Sulphur Mountain, is noted for its diversity of flora and fauna. The sounds here are those of nature—birdsong, the chattering of wildlife, the murmuring of Santa Paul Creek as it splashes through groves of California oak trees. Among the attractions are a bird aviary, a nature museum, a nature trail, horseshoe pits, a baseball diamond, and a volleyball/basketball court.

Camping

More than 220 tent and trailer campsites, some with full hookups, are available year-round; no showers.

Picnicking

Picnic tables are found throughout the park; some are situated near children's playgrounds, all are near restrooms and drinking water. Barbecue areas, some with electricity, are available for groups; advance reservations are required, and a fee is charged.

Fishing

One of the most popular fishing spots in the Ventura County park system, Santa Paula Creek is regularly stocked with trout.

How to Get There: Located in central Ventura County. From LA, take U.S. 101 north. Just before you reach the city of Ventura, head east on CA 126 to its junction with CA 150 in Santa Paula. Go north on CA 150 about 5½ miles to the park on the east side of the road.

Open daily, year-round, 7:30–5 October–April (7:30–7 on weekends in October, March, and April); 7:30 A.M.–9 P.M. May–September. Nominal vehicle entrance fee (less on weekdays); use fees for some facilities.

For Additional Information:
Ventura County Parks Department
800 S. Victoria Ave.
Ventura, CA 93009

805-654-3951

41. Stuart Orchids Nursery

Visitors are welcome to browse at the Stuart Nursery in Carpinteria, where more than 30,000 square feet of greenhouse space are devoted to the growing and selling of orchids. Hundreds of exquisite blooms of varied shapes, sizes, and colors are on display here.

How to Get There: From LA, drive north on U.S. 101 to the Linden Ave. exit in Carpinteria. Go north on Linden Ave. to Foothills Rd. and turn west to the nursery at 3376 Foothills Rd.

Open 8–4 Monday–Friday, 10–4 Saturday, and noon–4 Sunday; closed major holidays. Free group tours may be arranged by calling in advance.

For Additional Information:
Stuart Orchids
3376 Foothills Rd.
Carpinteria, CA 93013

805-684-5448

42. Tapia County Park

Tapia Park encompasses only 95 acres, but is one of the most popular units in the Santa Monica Mountains National Recreation Area (described elsewhere). It nestles in a shaded canyon against a backdrop of soaring mountain peaks, rolling hills, and groves of oak trees. In the southern part of the park, Malibu Creek meanders past banks where tall cottonwoods and willows shade the ground and offer refuge to many species of birds. Visitors skip rocks on the stream's surface and wade in its cool waters. Movie companies also find Tapia Park inviting and sometimes shoot films here. Unless you enjoy crowds, the best time to visit is on weekdays.

Hiking and Horseback Riding

Hiking and equestrian trails wind through the park and follow the banks of Malibu Creek.

Picnicking

Picnickers will find tables with grills and a sports field where they can work up an appetite or work off a feast.

How to Get There: Located in western Los Angeles County, just south of Malibu Creek State Park (described elsewhere). From LA, go north and west on U.S. 101 to Las Virgines–Malibu Canyon Rd. Turn south and go approximately 5 miles (crossing over Mulholland Hwy. and passing the entrance to Malibu Creek State Park along the way) to Tapia Park on the west side of the road. Parking on site.

Open daily, year-round, during daylight hours. Free.

For Additional Information:
County of Los Angeles
Dept. of Parks & Recreation
433 S. Vermont Ave.
Los Angeles, CA 90020

213-738-2961

Santa Monica Mountains National Recreation Area
22900 Ventura Blvd.
Woodland Hills, CA 91364

818-888-3770

Tapia County Park
844 N. Las Virgines Rd.
Calabasas, CA 91302

818-346-5008

43. Topanga State Park

Topanga State Park is a vast, virtually untouched wilderness that lies almost entirely within the boundaries of Los Angeles City. Within its 9,000-acre sprawl are deep canyons, craggy ridgetops, rock outcroppings, oak woodlands, chaparral-covered slopes, a small stream edged by lush vegetation in the spring, caves that offer cool shelter on hot days, a rugged terrain that ranges from 200 feet to 2,100 feet above sea level, and some spectacular views from atop summits that are among the highest in the Santa Monica Mountains. The park is a unit of the Santa Monica Mountains National Recreation Area (described elsewhere).

Hiking and Horseback Riding

Thirty-five miles of hiking and equestrian trails wind through the park. Be prepared to do some climbing. A 9-mile trail leads from Topanga State Park to adjacent Will Rogers State Historic Park (described elsewhere); it's possible to hike the trail either way, but an 1,800-foot drop in elevation makes it much easier to hike from Topanga to Rogers than vice versa. A nature trail at park headquarters follows a 1-mile loop; pick up a printed brochure for a self-guided walk or make arrangements in advance for a guided tour.

Picnicking

A picnic area with drinking water and restrooms is located next to the park office.

How to Get There: From downtown LA, take I-10 west to CA 1 (Pacific Coast Hwy.). Continue west on CA 1 to Topanga Canyon Blvd. (CA 27) and turn north to Entrada Rd. Turn east and follow Entrada, staying always to the left, until you come to the park entrance gate. Parking on site.

Open daily, year-round; 8–5 weekdays and 8–7 weekends during summer months, 8–5 during winter months; may be closed during high fire danger periods, particularly in late summer and fall. Nominal parking fee.

For Additional Information:
Topanga State Park
20825 Entrada Rd.
Topanga, CA 90290

213-455-2465
818-706-1310

Will Rogers State Historic Park
14253 Sunset Blvd.
Pacific Palisades, CA 90272

213-454-8212

California Department of Parks & Recreation
Santa Monica Mountains Area Headquarters
2860-A Camino Dos Rios
Newbury Park, CA 91320

818-706-1310
805-499-2112

Santa Monica Mountains National Recreation Area
22900 Ventura Blvd.
Woodland Hills, CA 91364

818-888-3770

44. Tule Elk State Reserve

Until the early 1800s, tule elk by the thousands
roamed California's great Central Valley. Then the in-
flux of people began in earnest, and the elk began
succumbing to hunters and the loss of natural habitat.
In 1874, one year after the California legislature
banned all elk hunting, only one pair of elk was
known to survive. Efforts to preserve the species continue to this day, but although small herds currently
exist in the wild in California, the amount of suitable
habitat is declining and the tule elk remains one of
the rarest mammals in the world.

The smallest of the three kinds of elk native to western North America, the male tule may weigh up to
550 pounds and stand slightly taller than 4 feet at the
shoulder. About forty of these unusual animals wander freely on the 953 acres of Tule Elk State Reserve
in the San Joaquin Valley. When enough natural food
is available, the herd sustains itself by foraging on the
vast stretches of flat, open grassland. During the dry
season (about May through February), supplemental
feedings are usually necessary. Then the herd is fed
each day between 2 and 3 P.M., within sight of a 5-
acre public viewing area, giving visitors a good opportunity to see the elks close-up. If you want to see
newborn calves, come in late April or early May.

It's a good idea to bring binoculars along on any
visit in case the elk are out to pasture. A caretaker
lives on the property and is often on hand to answer
questions. A very informative park brochure is available for a nominal fee.

Picnicking

A few picnic tables, along with restrooms and drinking water, dot the lawn in the viewing area.

How to Get There: Located in western Kern County,
about 25 miles west of Bakersfield. From LA, go north

on I-5 to the Stockdale Hwy. exit. Turn west onto
Stockdale Hwy., proceed about 1½ miles to Morris
Rd., and turn south. (Morris Rd. may not have a sign
to identify it.) Follow Morris Rd. to Station Rd., turn
west and proceed a short distance to the reserve entrance on the southern side of the road. Look for reserve signs in the area.

Open 8 A.M.—sunset daily. Free.

For Additional Information:
Tule Elk State Reserve
Route 1, Box 42
Buttonwillow, CA 93206

805-765-5004

South Valley Area Office
California Department of Parks and Recreation
Route 1, Box 42
Buttonwillow, CA 93206

805-765-5004

45. UCLA Gardens

Visitors to the University of California at Los Angeles
may see many unusual and exotic plants as they stroll
about the 411-acre campus. The beautifully landscaped grounds contain more than 370 species of
flora.

Tucked away in a canyon at the campus's southeastern corner are the 8-acre Mildred E. Mathias Botanical Gardens, where some 4,000 species of exotic
and native plants have been skillfully laid out to re-
semble a natural environment. The more mature specimens, grown huge with age, lend an aura of majesty
to the area. An adjacent herbarium contains an additional 250,000 plant specimens.

Art complements nature in the Franklin D. Murphy
Sculpture Garden, an outdoor museum where nearly
seventy sculptures adorn a 5-acre park. In the Geog-
raphy wing of Bunche Hall, which overlooks the
sculpture garden, you'll find a charming enclosed garden filled with tropical palms and other greenery.

The UCLA Japanese Garden, which lies off-campus,
is a jewel on a lush green hillside. It covers just one

acre, but is everything a Japanese garden should be—serene, esthetically pleasing, inspiring. Zigzagging paths lead past authentic Japanese plantings and artifacts imported from Japan to a bathhouse, teahouse, and shrine; Japanese maples whisper in the breeze; koi swim in shaded ponds studded with water lilies.

How to Get There: Located in western Los Angeles, just west of Beverly Hills. From downtown LA, go west on I-10 to I-405 (San Diego Fwy.). Take I-405 north to Wilshire Blvd. and turn east. Proceed on Wilshire Blvd. to Westwood Blvd. and turn north. Westwood Blvd. leads to LeConte Ave., which forms part of the southern boundary of the UCLA campus. Continue north across LeConte Ave. onto the campus (Westwood Blvd. now becomes Westwood Plaza) and proceed to the information booth on Westwood Plaza just north of Circle Drive South. Free maps of the campus are available here.

The entrance to the Mathias Botanical Gardens is located at the northwest corner of the intersection of Hilgard and LeConte Aves. (near the southeast corner of the campus). A trail booklet for self-guided tours is available at the garden office in the Botany Building, which stands near the garden's northern boundary. Garden open 8–4 daily; free.

The Murphy Sculpture Garden is located in the campus's northeast corner, just west of Circle Drive East. Bunche Hall stands near the garden's southern border. Garden open daily during daylight hours; free.

Parking on and around the campus is very limited Monday–Saturday; visitors may purchase campus parking permits on a daily basis subject to availability. Inquire at any information booth. Parking is usually readily available on Sundays.

Each spring and fall, UCLA sponsors free Green Thumb tours; qualified guides focus on campus landscaping, trees, and shrubs. Inquire at the Visitors Center in Dodd Hall; it's open 8–5 Monday–Friday.

The Japanese Garden lies north of the campus in Bel Air. Exit from the campus on Stone Canyon Dr. (located in the campus's northeast corner) and cross over Sunset Blvd., which forms the campus's northern boundary. Stone Canyon Dr. becomes Stone Canyon Rd. north of Sunset Blvd. Proceed north on Stone Canyon Rd., past the Bel Air Country Club, to Bellagio Rd. and turn west. The garden is located at 10619 Bellagio Rd., on the north side of the street. Free; self-guided and group tours available, but reservations are essential for either. Limited free parking at garden.

For Additional Information:
UCLA Visitors Center
100 Dodd Hall
405 Hilgard Ave.
Los Angeles, CA 90024

213-825-4574
213-206-8147

46. Ventura's Monarchs

Each winter, millions of Monarch butterflies descend upon Ventura and the surrounding countryside. They are part of the grandest insect spectacle on earth—a mass migration in which virtually all individuals in the population take part.

Coming from as far away as Canada, the orange and black butterflies return each year to winter in their favorite groves of cypress, eucalyptus, and pine along the California coast. Ventura's monarchs begin arriving in mid-October and are nearly gone by mid-March, with the greatest concentration present from mid-November to early January. On cool, cloudy days, they roost in area trees with wings folded, but on warm, sunny days, they spread their gossamer wings and flutter about the groves. It is a sight that even the most jaded of spectators will never forget.

How to Get There: To reach Ventura from LA, go northwest on U.S. 101, which passes through Ventura. The butterflies seem to favor the eucalyptus trees along Vista del Mar Dr. near the Pierpont Inn and the cypress trees at Seaside Wilderness Park (a nearly impenetrable area adjacent to Emma Wood State Beach that's known locally as "Hobo Jungle"), but the Ventura Visitors & Convention Bureau can advise you of the best areas in which to view the butterflies at any given time. The Bureau also gives out free literature about the Monarch.

For Additional Information:
Ventura Visitors & Convention Bureau
785 S. Seaward Ave.
Ventura, CA 93001

805-648-2075

47. Wattles Garden Park

This charming and tranquil 49-acre park is one of the lesser-known attractions of Hollywood and therefore rarely crowded. A private estate from the turn of the century until 1968, the park contains the mansion and remnants of formal gardens that once belonged to the Gurdon Wattles family. Visitors will see a Japanese teahouse with a miniature garden (given to the city of Los Angeles by its Japanese sister city, Nagoya), a second Japanese garden that includes a stream shared by carp and aquatic plants, and a notable stand of mature date palms. From its southern border along Hollywood Boulevard, the park climbs upward into the Hollywood Hills (the name given to the Santa Monica Mountains that lie within Hollywood). A hike through the native flora on the undeveloped northernmost hillside takes you to The Crest, an observation point 950 feet above sea level.

How to Get There: From LA, go north on U.S. 101 (Hollywood Fwy.) to Hollywood Blvd. and turn west. At the corner of Hollywood Blvd. and Curson Ave. (the park's southwest corner), turn north to the park's entrance gate at 1824 N. Curson Ave. on the east side of the street. Park on Curson Ave.

Open daily, year-round, during daylight hours. Free.

For Additional Information:
City of Los Angeles
Department of Recreation & Parks
200 N. Main St., 13th Floor
Los Angeles, CA 90012

213-485-5515 (General information)
213-876-9911 (Wattles Park)
213-485-4825

48. Will Rogers State Historic Park

On a hilltop in Pacific Palisades, overlooking the Pacific Ocean, lies the former home of the late Will Rogers. The 187-acre ranch and its buildings are maintained by the state just as they were when the beloved cowboy philosopher and his family lived there.

In the stables just north of the main house are polo ponies, used in games played year-round on the ranch's polo field. Riding trails laid out by Rogers himself wind among hills covered with native brush and eucalyptus.

Among the other facilities are a Visitors Center, where you'll see a short film on Rogers's life, and a nature center (open on weekends). You may also tour the humorist's thirty-one-room house, still filled with his possessions, and take an audio tour of the grounds.

Hiking and Horseback Riding

A nature trail for hikers only begins near the nature center. Trails used by both hikers and equestrians lead into the hills behind the ranch house. The trail to Inspiration Point and its view of Santa Monica Bay is an easy trek that totals 2 miles. A more strenuous trail, 6 miles round-trip, climbs a ridge line between two canyons, affording some marvelous views. Hikers and riders may also follow a spur trail into Topanga State Park (described elsewhere), which adjoins the northern and eastern boundaries of Rogers Park. The climb is a steep one, however, with a gain in elevation of some 1,800 feet, so most people prefer to arrange a shuttle and hike one-way from Topanga to Rogers. Equestrians must bring their own horses; the stables at Rogers Park are reserved for polo ponies.

Picnicking

A small family picnic area with tables is located east of Rogers's home.

How to Get There: Located in western Los Angeles, within the boundaries of the Santa Monica Mountains National Recreation Area (described elsewhere). From downtown LA, go west on I-10 to I-405. Take I-405 north to Sunset Blvd. and turn west to park on the north side of Sunset Blvd. Look for sign; parking on site.

Open daily, year-round, except January 1, Thanksgiving, December 25. Park open 8–7 May–October, 8–5 rest of year; home open 10–5 daily. Polo games are free and are usually played every Saturday afternoon, weather permitting; if you want to be sure of seeing a game, however, it's best to call and verify the schedule before your visit. Nominal parking fee.

For Additional Information:
Will Rogers State Historic Park
14253 Sunset Blvd.
Pacific Palisades, CA 90272
213-454-8212

California Department of Parks & Recreation
Santa Monica Mountains Area Headquarters
2860-A Camino Dos Rios
Newbury Park, CA 91320
818-706-1310
805-499-2112

Santa Monica Mountains National Recreation Area
22900 Ventura Blvd.
Woodland Hills, CA 91364
818-888-3770

49. Zond's Victory Garden Wind Farm

It is both eerie and beautiful—the ceaseless song of the wind as it sweeps across the high ridges of the Tehachapi Mountains. For many years, in this lonely spot 5,000 feet above sea level, it was the only sound that could be heard.

On Christmas Eve 1981, however, a new sound invaded these mountains—the rhythmic pounding of the wind turbine. It was the beginning of California's first independent wind farm, owned by Zond Systems, Inc., and operated under contract to Southern California Edison. Today, there are 103 of these contemporary windmills—metal towers of various heights, each topped with three rotor blades, that capture the wind and convert it to electricity.

Visitors are welcome at this 750-acre site, where you can drive to within 100 feet of the turbines. A self-service information center explains the facility's operations, and, as a bonus, there's an extraordinary view of the Mojave Desert and distant mountain ranges.

How to Get There: Located in south central Kern County and southeast of the town of Tehachapi. From LA, drive north on I-5 to CA 14 (Antelope Valley Fwy.) and turn northeast. Proceed on CA 14 to the town of Mojave, and turn west onto Oak Creek Rd. Go a few miles to the wind farm on the north side of Oak Creek Rd.

Open 9–5 daily. Free.

For Additional Information:
Zond Systems, Inc.
P.O. Box 1910
13000 Jameson Rd.
Tehachapi, CA 93561

805-822-6835

II

East by
Northeast

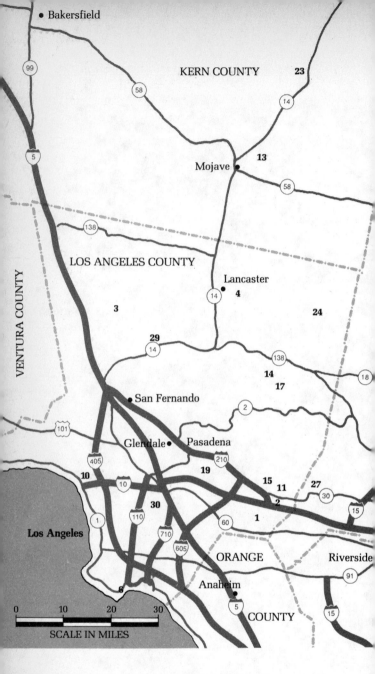

II: East by Northeast

1. Adobe de Palomares
2. Alf Museum
3. Angeles National Forest
4. Antelope Valley Wildflower and Wildlife Sanctuaries
5. Big Bear Valley Preserve
6. Cabrillo Beach and Marine Museum
7. Calico Early Man Site
8. California Aqueduct Bikeway
9. California Desert Preserve
10. Charmlee County Park
11. Claremont Tree Walks
12. Creosote Clone Preserve
13. Desert Tortoise Natural Research Area
14. Devil's Punchbowl County Regional Park

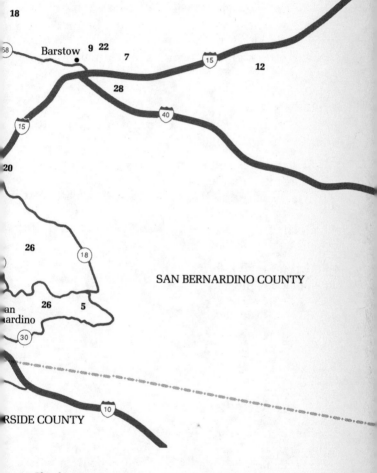

18

58 Barstow **9 22** **7** 15 **12**

28

15

20

26 18

SAN BERNARDINO COUNTY

an
ardino **26** **5**

30

RSIDE COUNTY 10

1. Adobe de Palomares

One of the most complete California restorations is the Adobe de Palomares in Pomona, originally built in 1854 with sun-dried adobe clay bricks. In the lovely, tree-shaded park that surrounds it are palm trees more than 100 years old, wisteria vines that date back nearly a century, and grapevines grown from cuttings taken from vines at the San Gabriel Mission in the 1850s. Bright flowers dot the lawns most of the year. It was also here that the infamous Bermuda grass was introduced to southern California. A former owner of the adobe brought it to his home from the Caribbean.

Picnicking

Picnic tables are located in picturesque settings among the grapevines.

How to Get There: From LA, drive east on I-10 (San Bernardino Fwy.) to the Garey Ave. exit. Head north on Garey to Arrow Highway, then turn east to the adobe on the north (left) side of the highway.

Open 2–5 daily except Monday. Grounds free; nominal admission fee to adobe.

For Additional Information:
Adobe de Palomares
491 E. Arrow Hwy.
Pomona, CA 91767

714-620-2300

2. Alf Museum

Youngsters of all ages—and parents, too—will enjoy the Raymond M. Alf Museum just east of Los Angeles. Located on the grounds of Webb School, a college-prep institution for boys, the museum is a repository for artifacts found by Dr. Alf and his students during several paleontological digs. Exhibits include a peccary skull that's 15 million years old, fossil footprints, fossils that depict mammalian history, ancient Egyptian relics, and an assortment of bones.

How to Get There: From LA, take I-10 (San Bernardino Fwy.) east to the Indian Hill Blvd. exit near

Claremont. Go north on Indian Hill Blvd. to Base Line Rd. (CA 30), then west to the museum at 1175 W. Base Line Rd. Parking on site.

Open 8–4 Monday–Saturday, by advance appointment only. Free.

For Additional Information:
Raymond M. Alf Museum
1175 W. Base Line Rd.
Claremont, CA 91711

714-624-2798

3. Angeles National Forest

On the doorstep of greater Los Angeles is America's most popular national forest—the Angeles—consisting of some 693,000 acres principally in the San Gabriel Mountain range. The boundaries along the south side of the forest, which ironically includes two entire wilderness areas and a portion of another, are marked with real estate development and the intensive expansion of population growth.

It is little wonder the Angeles National Forest, for those who must have space in order to breathe, has become a veritable mecca to thousands of people living all over southern California. It encompasses spectacular scenery, is home to a variety of wildlife, and during winter and spring (when the air is clear enough to see) provides a scenic backdrop to the city with snow-capped mountains and flowing streams.

Not so many years ago, the mountainous terrain of the Angeles was home to the endangered California condor, which was frequently seen soaring along the thermal updrafts from the San Gabriels. But that was fifty years ago, not today. The last stronghold of the condor was in the neighboring Los Padres National Forest, and today no condors remain in the wild.

There is a great variety of wildlife living in the Angeles, however, including many seldom if ever seen, such as mountain lion, lynx, fox, mule deer, black bear, desert bighorn sheep, and a variety of owls and raptors. Golden and bald eagles are not uncommon and there are many songbirds, squirrels, and raccoons as well as rodents. Many of these, of course, are found only in more remote areas; others come out only at night.

Although the Angeles is designated national forest, it is mostly vegetated with chaparral. Sycamore, cottonwoods, mesquite, paloverde, and, at higher elevations, juniper, piñon, fir, and ponderosa pine and the ancient limber pines are found. Most of the limber pines, which are identified by their rich deep cinnamon color, are found near the summit of Mt. Baden-Powell, named after Lord Baden-Powell, founder of the Boy Scouts of America. Many of these date back to the time of Christ; others are a mere 1,000 years old.

You can see the 9,399-foot Mt. Baden-Powell, which incidentally is almost a thousand feet shorter than Mt. San Antonio–Old Baldy, which rises above 10,000 feet within the Sheep Mountain Wilderness area, as you drive along the Angeles Crest Highway. In fact, this road is highly recommended for your introduction to the Angeles. From it, you can view much of the spectacular scenery that makes this particular national forest so rewarding. From the community of LaCanada nestled in the foothills of the San Gabriels, SR 2 (the Angeles Crest Highway) leads up to Big Pines. Not only is it a study in scenic territory, it also is a laboratory on change of vegetation with elevation. Possibly you may even see desert bighorn sheep on more distant slopes of the mountains as you travel this route. Spring and fall are the very best times to take the road.

In the spring, the gentle slopes of some of the lesser mountain terrain such as that on the Saugus District are dressed with veritable carpets of wildflowers, especially lupines, larkspur, and California poppies. The desert slopes of the Tujunga and Valyermo districts of the forest provide special exhibits of the awesome geological forces that shaped the land. Several earthquake faults still are found here, but the Pacoima Fault located near the little community of Pacoima is most prominent. It's directly northeast of the highly populated San Fernando Valley. The most famous earthquake fault in all of North America, however—the San Andreas—barely gets into the Angeles Forest. It's more part of the landscape of the neighboring San Bernardino National Forest than it is the Angeles. It does slice through the extreme northeast section of the Saugus and Valyermo districts before making its way southeast to the Salton Sea and the Imperial Valley.

The two wilderness areas totally within the Angeles are the San Gabriel, covering some 36,000 acres, and Sheep Mountain, containing some 44,000 acres. A third—the Cucamonga—is smaller and shared with the San Bernardino National Forest. The San Gabriel was designated wilderness long ago (1932), but Sheep Mountain was set aside only in 1984. Both offer equally true wilderness experiences.

The San Gabriel encompasses extremely rugged terrain, ranging in elevation from 1,600 to 8,200 feet. Lower elevations are covered with dense chaparral, which rapidly changes to pine- and fir-covered slopes, high peaks, and meadows of wildflowers during the warm weather months. Only experienced hikers are advised to enter the San Gabriel Wilderness; this is not so true of Sheep Mountain, which accommodates all levels of hiking from novice to expert. While Sheep Mountain elevations extend to well over 10,000 feet, the terrain is not so rugged. All of the descriptions attributed to the San Gabriel apply to Sheep Mountain and Cucamonga as well.

Hiking

Several hundred miles of hiking trails await you in the Angeles National Forest. Among them are portions of the Pacific Crest National Scenic Trail, which extends the breadth of the nation from Mexico to Canada. It enters the Angeles near Wright Mountain and wanders across the high country to the Angeles Crest Highway. Part of the route it takes across the national forest parallels the San Andreas Fault before heading across the Mojave Desert toward the high Sierra Nevada Mountains. Four other national hiking trails are part of the Angeles. They are the High Desert National Recreation Trail, West Fort NRT, Gabrielino NRT, and Silver Moccasin NRT, named after the merit badge Boy Scouts receive for making this 52-mile hike.

The wilderness areas are especially attractive for hiking, since their trails lead you away from off-road vehicle areas, highways, and the sights and sounds that go with high-density populated areas. Special maps and literature are available from the national forest on hiking these areas, as well as other hiking trails scattered throughout the forest. Some of the more notable ones are the Bear Creek Trail and Devil's Canyon Trail leading into the San Gabriel, the East Fork and Mine Gulch trails leading through the Sheep

Mountain Wilderness, the Windy Gap Trail in the Crystal Lake area, and the Glen Camp Trail, which only extends some seven miles and is an easy day hike. Several of the trails lead out of family campgrounds. Keep in mind that the trails into the wilderness areas require a permit, available free of charge from the Visitors' Centers or a ranger station. Also keep in mind that this is rattlesnake country. This is their territory so if you encounter one, just back off and allow the critter to move on its way before going on yours. Be alert at all times for their presence. A snakebite kit in your first-aid pack is advisable.

If hiking during winter months, be extremely careful of crossing snow areas on steep slopes. Quite often, snow melts, then refreezes, and additional snow settles on top of the ice. To try hiking across such areas is very dangerous. Aside from the hazards imposed by cold weather, winter is a most rewarding time to hike in the forest and a very good time for taking photographs too.

Camping

Extensive camping opportunities exist in the Angeles, ranging from padded level recreational vehicle sites to primitive hike-in campgrounds deep in the wilderness. Most areas are open on a year-round basis and on a first-come basis. Some group camps may be reserved. Some are fee areas, others free. While recreational vehicles are welcome at several locations, there are no electric, water, or sewage hookups. Keep in mind that fire permits are required, and, during the dry season, which is usually late spring until the first soaking rains of winter, no fires are permitted. Fire is an extreme hazard throughout the area much of the year because of the dry climate.

Between October 15 and May 15, be sure to check with the Forest Service on whether the facility you wish to visit is actually open. Some literature is available from the forest headquarters or any district ranger station on camping in the Angeles. Plan accordingly.

Fishing

Two lakes within the Angeles offer superb fishing in the early spring and late fall—Pyramid Lake and Castaic Lake. Striped bass, rainbow and brown trout, and catfish may be found. Boats are permitted on both lakes. At Crystal, Jackson, and Elizabeth lakes, you may fish from the bank for rainbow trout. Several streams including the North and West Forks of the San Gabriel River, Big and Little Rock creeks, Big Tujunga River, and Bouquet Canyon are stocked with rainbow trout by the California Fish & Game Department. A state fishing license is required.

Canoeing

Canoeing and boating are permitted on both Pyramid and Castaic lakes in the forest, but be cautious of heavy visitor season—mid-May to mid-September, particularly on weekends. Weekdays can offer pleasant canoeing experiences year-round.

How to Get There: The Angeles is divided primarily into two sections and lies both north and northeast of the greater Los Angeles area. I-5 leads through portions of it north of the city. SR 14 leading east off I-5 also parallels portions of the national forest. Watch for signs directing you to the Angeles National Forest.

For Additional Information:
Forest Supervisor
Angeles National Forest
701 N. Santa Anita Ave.
Arcadia, CA 91006
818-577-0050

4. Antelope Valley Wildflower and Wildlife Sanctuaries

The Los Angeles County Department of Parks and Recreation administers eight wildflower and wildlife sanctuaries in the Antelope Valley, a portion of the Mojave Desert that spills across the northern part of the county. Totaling more than 2,100 acres, these preserves present a multihued panorama of spring wildflowers that lures thousands of visitors each year. The shimmering show begins with a golden splash of California poppies around mid-March, peaks in April, and continues into June—a pageant of riotous colors and unusual blooms.

You may also spot some of the desert's wildlife—golden eagles, marsh hawks, ravens, chuckwallas, sidewinder and Mojave rattlesnakes, roadrunners, and desert tortoises.

If you want to avoid the crowds during peak blooming periods, it's best to come on a weekday. You may also enjoy visiting here other times of the year to experience the many moods of the desert. Although the landscape is less colorful in other seasons, there is always something of interest to observe.

The sanctuaries are neither developed nor staffed, but special wildflower programs are conducted in the spring. The eight preserves are known as the Butte Valley and Phacelia wildflower sanctuaries and the Alpine Butte, Gerhardy, Mescal, Big Rock Creek, Tujunga, and Payne wildlife sanctuaries.

How to Get There: Located in northeastern Los Angeles County, east of CA 14. Since these sanctuaries are not easily located, it's best to contact the Department of Parks & Recreation for exact directions before your visit.

Open daily, at all times, throughout the year. Free.

For Additional Information:
Natural Areas Division
County of Los Angeles
Department of Parks & Recreation
433 S. Vermont
Los Angeles, CA 90012

213-738-2961

Wildlife/Wildflowers information:

805-259-7721

5. Big Bear Valley Preserve

At the eastern end of Big Bear Valley in San Bernardino County is the world's largest undisturbed stretch of pavement plain, a 124-acre remnant of the ice age that was pushed to the surface by alternate freezing and thawing during the Pleistocene epoch. The soil is a mix of alkaline clay and pebbles of sarragossa quartz that inhibits the establishment of pine seedlings, thus creating a treeless pocket within the pine forest that surrounds it. Lying at an elevation of 6,720 feet above sea level, the preserve has become a refuge for an amazing array of alpine plants. At least fourteen types of wildflowers that are rare and endangered in California thrive here, and ten of these, found within the preserve and a 15-mile radius from its boundaries, grow nowhere else in the world.

Baldwin Lake, which adjoins the preserve's southern border, is all that remains of a huge lake that covered Big Bear Valley in prehistoric times. Each year, thousands of migratory waterfowl winter here, and bald eagles come to prey on the mud hens. Nine different species of sparrows, including the rare Nevada sage sparrow, nest in the area, and in the spring, the meadowlarks and killdeer fill the air with their music.

Big Bear Valley Preserve is managed by the California Field Office of The Nature Conservancy.

Hiking

The opportunities for hiking here are virtually limitless. Trails through the preserve are augmented by the trail system of the adjacent San Bernardino National Forest (described elsewhere) and by the nearby Pacific Crest National Scene Trail (also described elsewhere). Visitors are asked not to wander randomly across preserve lands, as the rare plants are particularly vulnerable to trampling. Free guided tours of the rare plant communities are offered on a regular basis.

Camping

No camping is allowed on the preserve itself, but arrangements for camping in the national forest may be made at the U.S. Forest Service Ranger Station about 4 miles east of Fawnskin on CA 38. Camping is also permitted at designated areas along the Pacific Crest National Scenic Trail, which runs in a generally east-west direction just north of the preserve. All campsites are primitive, and you'll have to bring your own drinking water.

How to Get There: From LA, take I-10 east to I-15E and turn north to the CA 18/30 turnoff in San Bernardino. Follow CA 18/30 east, continuing on CA 30 after it separates from CA 18 to CA 330 and turn north to CA 18. Follow CA 18 east, through the city of Big Bear Lake and beyond Big Bear Lake itself. When you reach

Baldwin Lake, start looking for Holcomb Valley Rd., a paved road that runs north from CA 18. Turn left on Holcomb Valley Rd. for approximately 100 yards to a dirt parking lot. It's a good idea to carry chains with you on a winter visit; roads in the vicinity of Big Bear Lake are often snowbound and icy at that time of year.

Open daily, year-round, during daylight hours. Free.

For Additional Information:
Preserve Manager
Big Bear Valley Preserve
Box 1418
Sugarloaf, CA 92386

714-866-4190

California Field Office
The Nature Conservancy
785 Market St.
San Francisco, CA 94103

415-777-0487

The Nature Conservancy
Southern California Chapter Project Office
849 S. Broadway, 6th Floor
Los Angeles, CA 90014

213-622-6594

6. Cabrillo Beach and Marine Museum

The primary attraction at Cabrillo Beach, the Cabrillo Marine Museum, has been a favorite on the LA scene since the 1920s. A showcase for southern California marine life, the museum offers such exhibits as an 1,100-pound leatherneck turtle, a 28-foot skeleton of a young gray whale, a pile of whalebones that you can rummage through to your heart's delight, a simulated tide pool, more than 15,000 seashells, and some thirty aquariums, watery homes for a fascinating variety of sea creatures and plants.

The museum also sponsors an array of special events—whale-watching boat trips, Channel Island boat trips, nocturnal grunion programs, guided tide-pool tours at the Point Fermin Marine Life Refuge, which lies between Cabrillo Beach and Point Fermin to the west, and many more. Call for a schedule. You may also pick up a brochure on tide-pool biology at the museum and explore the tide pools on your own.

Water Sports

A special area on the ocean is reserved for surfers; swimmers use a stillwater beach inside the breakwater. Divers are intrigued by offshore kelp beds. Lifeguard in summer.

Fishermen angle in the surf for spotfin and yellowfin croakers, barred perch, and corbina or from a 1,200-foot public pier for the same species plus barracuda, bonito, halibut, jacksmelt, and mackerel. A free concrete boat-launching ramp has four lanes; bait shop, but no rental boats.

Picnicking

A shaded picnic area on the beach has fire rings and barbecue pits. Nearby are a snack bar, volleyball courts, and a children's playground.

How to Get There: Located in south central Los Angeles County. From downtown LA, go south on I-110 (Harbor Fwy.) until it ends in San Pedro at Gaffey St. Continue south on Gaffey St. to 22nd St., turn east to Pacific Ave., then south to Stephen White Dr. (36th St.). Follow Stephen White Dr. east to Cabrillo Beach and the museum (located next to the parking lot).

Beach and fishing pier open 7 A.M.–10 P.M. daily, year-round. Vehicle parking fee. Museum open 10 A.M.–5 P.M. Tuesday–Sunday, year-round; museum is free, but there's a charge to park.

For Additional Information:
Cabrillo Marine Museum
3720 Stephen White Dr.
San Pedro, CA 90731

213-548-7562 (Museum)
213-832-1179 (Life Guards)

City of Los Angeles Department of Recreation &
  Parks
200 N. Main St., 13th Floor
Los Angeles, CA 90012

213-485-5515

7. Calico Early Man Site

In the Mojave Desert, just two miles north of I-15, is one of the most exciting archaeological finds of all time. The Calico Early Man Site (known locally as the Calico Dig) places man on this continent some 200,000 years ago, making this site a good 50,000 years older than any other site in the Western Hemisphere.

When prehistoric man lived here, this area was lush and green, and the abundant rainfall was captured in a 250-square-mile lake. A massive earthquake eventually reshaped the land, allowing all water to drain from the lake. In the late 1950s, a survey of the ancient lake bed turned up some human artifacts. This led to the 1958 discovery of the nearby Calico site, believed to be the workshop area in which these primitive people made their stone tools. Thus far, more than 12,000 prime-quality artifacts have been unearthed—anvils, cutting tools, hammerstones, scrapers for woodworking, burins for bone working, a circle of thirteen stones that once enclosed campfires, and many others.

So significant is the site that it is the only New World project ever undertaken by the late Dr. Louis Leakey. Dr. Leakey, noted for his famous early-man discoveries in East Africa, begin directing excavations here after his first visit to the site in 1963.

The Calico excavations, still going on, provide a unique outdoor museum of Pleistocene archaeology and geology. Many representative artifacts, as well as excavation tools and photos of the project at various stages, are displayed in Camp Leakey, an old prospector's cabin that serves as a Visitors Center.

If you're interested in paleontology, you might want to participate in the excavation of this site. The San Bernardino County Museum (see address at the end of this entry) includes up to twenty amateurs per dig in supervised digs conducted the second week of each month.

How to Get There: From LA, go east on I-10 to I-15, and take I-15 northeast through Barstow to the Minneola Rd. exit. (Ignore any signs directing you to Calico Ghost Town, a separate park that has nothing to do with the Early Man site.) From the Minneola Rd.

exit, signs will direct you north for two miles on a graded dirt road to the Calico Site's parking area.

Open 8–5 daily except Tuesday, year-round. Free.

For Additional Information:
Calico Early Man Site
c/o Regional Parks Department
San Bernardino County
825 E. Third St.
San Bernardino, CA 92415

714-387-2594

Desert Information Ctr.
Bureau of Land Management
831 Barstow Rd.
Barstow, CA 92311

619-256-8617

Friends of the Calico Early Man Site, Inc.
P.O. Box 535
Yermo, CA 92398

(*no phone*)

San Bernardino County Museum
2024 Orange Tree Ln.
Redlands, CA 92373

714-825-4825

8. California Aqueduct Bikeway

Following paved service roads that border the open canals along the East Branch of the California Aqueduct, this 107-mile-long bikeway leads bicyclists and hikers through the solitary desert environment of the Antelope Valley, noted for its varied wildlife, its Joshua trees, and its magnificent displays of spring wildflowers. Travelers will also have the opportunity to view some of the geologic features created by the San Andreas Fault (described elsewhere), which parallels this section of the aqueduct.

Although no camping is permitted along the bikeway itself, campsites are available in several areas adjacent to the bikeway. Trailside rest stops, situated at intervals of approximately 10 miles, offer picnic tables, drinking water, toilets, and shade ramadas.

If you're planning to bike or hike any considerable distance, take along food and drink. Obtain a weather forecast before starting out, and request a free bikeway map from the State Department of Water Resources so that you will know in advance where all rest stops, exit roads, and nearby towns are located. In addition, bikers should take along spare bicycle parts.

Plans call for the bikeway to eventually be extended to a length of nearly 400 miles, following the aqueduct northward from Quail Lake into the San Joaquin Valley near San Francisco.

Fishing

Fishing is permitted along most of the bikeway. Angling for striped bass, bluegill, and catfish is especially good in the spring and fall.

How to Get There: Located in Los Angeles and San Bernardino counties. The bikeway follows a northwest/southeast route and may be entered from either terminus or from any of the numerous roads that cross it. Quail Lake, the northwestern terminus, may be reached by going north from LA on I-5 to CA 138 and turning east; the lake lies on the north side of CA 138 just east of the intersection of CA 138 and I-5. The bikeway begins at the northeast corner of a parking lot near the west end of Quail Lake. To reach the southeastern terminus, which lies just north of Silverwood Lake, proceed east from LA on I-10 to I-15. Take I-15 north to CA 138, and turn east to CA 173. Continue east on CA 173 to Las Flores Rd., then turn north to a parking lot on the east side of the road. The bikeway ends at the east side of Las Flores Rd. not far north of this parking lot.

Open daily, year-round, sunup to sundown. Free.

For Additional Information:
Department of Water Resources
Southern Field Division
P.O. Box 98
Castaic, CA 91310

805-257-3610

Palmdale Chamber of Commerce
38269 10th St. E.
Palmdale, CA 93550

805-273-3232

9. California Desert Preserve

The vast California desert, sprawling over more than 25 million acres, is one of the most extraordinary wilderness areas in the country. There is beauty here that takes your breath away, rare flora and fauna that live nowhere else on earth, a diversity of landscape that is incredible. Within the desert's boundaries are mountains, sand dunes as high as twenty-four-story buildings, unusual rock formations, rugged canyons, geologic features exposed by the rumblings of a network of earthquake faults, areas rich with fossils, caves, hot springs, cool pools of water, marshes, and a river that appears and disappears several times along its meandering way. A creosote bush in Johnson Valley is believed to be more than 11,500 years old—possibly the oldest-known living plant in the world.

Man has come and gone through the years, leaving behind him ghost towns, abandoned mines, and old homesteads. Petroglyphs, pictographs, and intaglios are legacies of the Native Americans. One archaeological excavation has uncovered the oldest-known human settlement in the Western Hemisphere, placing man in the Americas some 200,000 years ago.

Much of the desert lies within the 100-mile radius prescribed for this book, and some of its wonders, such as the San Andreas Fault, the Salton Sea, the Joshua Tree National Monument, and others, are described elsewhere. You can learn more about all the desert has to offer at the Barstow Way Station Visitor Center. Operated by the Bureau of Land Management, a division of the U.S. Department of the Interior which manages more than 12 million acres of public lands in the California Desert, it has a friendly staff that can give you directions to the various attractions, advise you where and what recreational activities are available, provide you with free maps and brochures, and keep you up-to-date on weather and road conditions (important considerations when you're traveling in the desert). The BLM plans to build nine other way stations elsewhere in the desert in the future.

How to Get There: The California Desert, which encompasses the Mojave Desert, the Sonoran Desert, and a small portion of the Great Basin Desert, lies east of Los Angeles; it stretches south to the Mexican border, north to the Inyo and Sequoia national forests, and east to the boundary lines of Arizona and Nevada. To reach the Barstow Way Station, located in the heart of the desert, go east from LA on I-10 to I-15. Take I-15 north to the Central Barstow exit, and follow signs to the Desert Information Ctr. at 831 Barstow Rd.

The Way Station is open 8–4:30 Monday–Friday, 9–5 Saturday and Sunday; closed Thanksgiving, December 25, January 1. Free; parking on site.

For Additional Information:
Desert Information Ctr.
Bureau of Land Management
831 Barstow Rd.
Barstow, CA 92311

619-256-8617

California Desert District Office
Bureau of Land Management
1695 Spruce St.
Riverside, CA 92507

714-351-6383
714-351-6394

10. Charmlee County Park

Perched on a hillside above the Pacific Coast Highway west of Los Angeles, this delightful park offers 460 acres of sprawling meadows, dense oak woodlands, and chaparral; it has one of the finest displays of spring wildflowers in southern California and magnificent views of the Pacific. Kite fliers launch gossamer crafts from blufftops some 1,300 feet above the ocean, and winter visitors sometimes spot migrating gray whales. Primarily undeveloped at this writing, Charmlee is little known and rarely crowded. Plans for the future include an information center, a walk-in tent camping area, and an equestrian trail. Contact the Los Angeles County Department of Parks & Recreation for the latest information about facilities.

Hiking
Hiking, via a network of trails and fire roads, is the main activity.

Picnicking

If you enjoy picnicking in solitude, complete with ocean view, this is the place for you. There are restrooms in the park, but you'll have to bring your own drinking water.

How to Get There: Located in westernmost Los Angeles county, within the boundaries of the Santa Monica Mountains National Recreation Area (described elsewhere). From LA, go west on I-10 to CA 1 (Pacific Coast Hwy.). Continue west on CA 1 to Encinal Canyon Rd., and turn north to park entrance on west side of road. Parking on site; if entrance gate is locked, park and walk in.

Open daily, year-round, during daylight hours. Free.

For Additional Information:
County of Los Angeles
Department of Parks & Recreation
433 S. Vermont Ave.
Los Angeles, CA 90020

213-738-2961

Santa Monica Mountains National Recreation Area
22900 Ventura Blvd.
Woodland Hills, CA 91364

818-888-3770

View from Charmlee County Park, Los Angeles County

11. Claremont Tree Walks

The pleasant community of Claremont, located at the base of Mount Baldy in the San Gabriel Mountains, is noted for its extensive collection of native and exotic trees. Some of the most outstanding specimens may be viewed by taking three easy walks in the older part of town and on the campuses of the Claremont Colleges (a complex of six separate liberal arts institutions).

Each of these trees is labeled and keyed to a list that provides common names, botanical names, and places of origin for the various species. You may purchase the list and a tree-tour map at several places in Claremont, including the Howard Johnson Motor Lodge on Indian Hill Blvd. just north of I-10.

How to Get There: From LA, drive east on I-10 to the Indian Hill Blvd. exit in Claremont and turn north. Proceed to the Howard Johnson Motor Lodge, or inquire locally about other places where a tree-tour map may be purchased.

For Additional Information:
Rancho Santa Ana Botanic Garden
1500 N. College Ave.
Claremont, CA 91711

714-626-1917
714-625-8767

Chamber of Commerce
Claremont City Hall
2nd & Harvard Sts.
Claremont, CA 91711

714-624-1681

Convention and Visitors Bureau
205 Yale Ave.
Claremont, CA 91711

714-621-9644

12. Creosote Clone Preserve

More than 11 millenniums ago, perhaps as long ago as the last stages of the last ice age, a single seed took root in the sands of the Mojave Desert. Today, the creosote bush to which that seed gave birth still thrives—an estimated 11,700 years old. It is the oldest known living organism on the planet.

Rather than producing a single bush that over the years grows in bulk, a creosote seedling clones itself. The lower stems of the original bush send out new branches that develop their own roots, creating a gradually expanding ring of bushes that encircles a stretch of bare soil where the older, interior portions of the plant have died off. As a ring spreads outward, it breaks the sand into fine particles that store water more efficiently than the coarser soil outside the ring, enabling the shrubs to better withstand droughts. Although creosote bushes grow only 4 or 5 feet tall and are somewhat scraggly-looking, they are among the hardiest of plants.

The ancient creosote bush that is protected in this 17-acre preserve, purchased by the Nature Conservancy in March 1985, is currently a 70-foot-long, 25-foot-wide ellipse. Known as King Clone, it was discovered in the mid-1970s by Dr. Frank Vasek, a botanist at the University of California at Riverside. Since the creosote bush is the most dominant plant species of our country's southwestern deserts, there is the tantalizing possibility that somewhere in the vast reaches of this arid landscape there grows an even older creosote bush, but until it is found, King Clone reigns as the granddaddy of them all.

How to Get There: Located in southeastern San Bernardino County in Johnson Valley. In order to protect this unique plant and the virtually untouched habitat in which it grows, visitation is restricted. Contact the following addresses for further details.

For Additional Information:
The Nature Conservancy
California Field Office
785 Market St.
San Francisco, CA 94103

415-777-0487

The Nature Conservancy
Southern California Chapter Project Office
213 Stearns Wharf
Santa Barbara, CA 93101

805-962-9111

Dr. Frank C. Vasek
Professor of Botany
Department of Botany & Plant Science
University of California
Riverside, CA 92521
714-787-1012

13. Desert Tortoise Natural Research Area

Once plentiful in the southwestern United States, the desert tortoise is now a threatened species. The Bureau of Land Management, which is in charge of much of the public lands in the California desert, has set aside a 38-square-mile area of prime tortoise habitat in an effort to assure the preservation of this species. Known as the Desert Tortoise Research Natural Area, it is currently a mix of federal and nonfederal lands.

The preserve contains the finest known populations of the desert tortoise, now designated California's state reptile. In parts of the natural area, there are as many as 200 tortoises per square mile. These intriguing reptiles have a life span of from sixty to eighty years, but only two to five out of every 100 born survive to maturity. About 2 inches long at birth, they continue to grow most of their lives, reaching lengths of up to 14 inches in midlife. Much of the year, perhaps six to nine months, the tortoises hibernate in underground burrows to protect themselves from temperature extremes. Sometime early in the spring, they emerge to feed upon the desert wildflowers that are their favorite food and to court before hot summer temperatures force them back to their subterranean homes.

The best time to visit here is from March through May, when more than 160 different types of wildflowers blanket the land and the tortoises are on the move. It's also a good time to observe some of the other wildlife that inhabits this part of the Mojave Desert—coyote, desert kit fox, chuckwalla, the rare Mojave ground squirrel, and many species of birds.

An interpretive center near the entrance to the natural area provides information about the desert and its inhabitants, as well as maps for the self-guiding nature trails. Bring your own drinking water; none is available at the preserve.

How to Get There: Located in the Mojave Desert in southeastern Kern County. From LA, drive north on I-5 to CA 14. Take CA 14 east and north through the town of Mojave. About 4 miles north of Mojave, turn east onto California City Blvd. and proceed for about 10 miles to the Randsburg-Mojave Rd. Turn northeast and continue on Randsburg-Mojave Rd. for about 5½ miles to the preserve entrance, which lies just off the road on the left side. Look for signs. Parking on site.

Open daily, year-round, during daylight hours. Admission is free, but the Desert Tortoise Preserve Committee, which is working in cooperation with The Nature Conservancy to purchase natural area lands that are still privately owned, needs and appreciates any donations.

For Additional Information:
Desert Tortoise Preserve Committee
P.O. Box 453
Ridgecrest, CA 93555

805-831-2325

California Desert District Office
Bureau of Land Management
1695 Spruce St.
Riverside, CA 92507

714-351-6394

California Field Office
The Nature Conservancy
785 Market St.
San Francisco, CA 94103

415-777-0487

14. Devil's Punchbowl County Regional Park

The rumblings of several earthquake faults, including the San Andreas (described elsewhere), created the stunning landscape that is the main attraction of this remote 1,310-acre park. Jutting up from a depression in the earth, named the Devil's Punchbowl partly because of its cuplike shape, is a jumble of enormous, dun-colored rock slabs that tilt every which way. They form a natural rock garden that extends 3 miles in length and is up to 1 mile wide. For 13 million years, since the rocks were first deposited here, they have been alternately compressed, folded, broken, faulted, and uplifted into the bizarre formations visitors see today. The ancient, fossil-studded rocks, the faults that cut through the park, and some hills just north of the Punchbowl that contain formations nearly 60 million years old make this whole area geologically intriguing.

During part of the year, a small stream makes its way through the maze of the punchbowl. Groves of manzanita, juniper, piñon, and many types of chaparral plants thrive among the rocks and provide sanctuary for the park's wildlife.

Near the rim of the Punchbowl is a Visitor Center with displays that explain the natural history of the area. Although the park is operated by the County of Los Angeles, it lies within the Angeles National Forest (described elsewhere), and 1,270 acres of this parkland are owned by the U.S. Forest Service.

Hiking

A milelong loop trail descends into the Punchbowl. The Piñon Pathway Nature Trail is about ⅓ of a mile long; a printed trail guide is available. Serious hikers may want to follow a park trail that joins an up-and-down route, 6 miles one way, to South Fork Campground in adjacent Angeles National Forest; before setting out on this longer trail, it's best to advise park or forest personnel of your plans. Hikers sometimes get lost here.

Picnicking

A shaded picnic area near the parking lot provides views of the Punchbowl as you eat; drinking water and restrooms are close at hand.

How to Get There: Located in east central Los Angeles County. From LA, go north on I-5 to CA 14 (Antelope Valley Fwy.), then go northeast on CA 14 to the Little Rock turnoff just beyond Vincent. Travel east on the turnoff (also known as Pearblossom Hwy.

and, for part of the route, as CA 138) through Little Rock and Pearblossom. Just beyond Pearblossom, look for the Devil's Punchbowl County Regional Park sign, turn south on Co. Rd. N-6, and follow N-6 to the park. Look for signs along the way. N-6 first follows Longview Rd./131st St. south, then jogs east on Fort Tejon Rd., then turns south again on Longview Rd./131st St., then turns east on Tumbleweed Rd. (also known as Devil's Punchbowl Rd.). Tumbleweed Rd. ends at the park. Parking on site.

Open daily, year-round, during daylight hours. Free.

For Additional Information:
Devil's Punchbowl County Regional Park
28000 Devil's Punchbowl Rd.
Pearblossom, CA 93553

805-944-2473

County of Los Angeles
Department of Parks & Recreation
433 S. Vermont Ave.
Los Angeles, CA 90020

213-738-2961

15. Glendora Bougainvillea

The largest growth of bougainvillea in the continental United States is located along the streets of Glendora. Although the magenta, scarlet, and purple blooms can be seen throughout the year, they are most profuse in December and from May through June. The flowering plants reach heights of 50 to 70 feet, engulfing the lower parts of the palm trees that line Bennett and Minnesota avenues, and sprawl approximately 600 feet along each thoroughfare. Dating back to the turn of the century, the bougainvilleas were designated a State Historic Landmark in 1978.

How to Get There: Located in the heart of Glendora. From downtown LA, go east on I-10 to I-605. Take I-605 north to I-210. Follow I-210 east to Grand Ave. in Glendora. Go north on Grand Ave. to Bennett Ave. and turn east to the corner of Bennett and Minnesota Aves.

For Additional Information:
Glendora Chamber of Commerce
224 N. Glendora Ave.
Glendora, CA 91740

818-963-4128

16. Glen Helen Regional Park

Set against a backdrop of towering mountains and chaparral-covered hills, Glen Helen Regional Park offers 500 acres of open water, grassy meadows and slopes, sycamore and alder groves, and wetlands. You can wander through a natural marsh accompanied by birdsong, frog croaks, and slithery rustles that signal the passage of unseen creatures through tall grasses. The summer air is sweet with the fragrance of wild mint, and buttercups brighten the spring landscape.

Hiking and Horseback Riding

A ½-mile-long ecology trail follows a boardwalk through the marsh; more footpaths wind through the meadows and across creeks and inlets. Horseback riders will also find trails to roam; horses may be rented or boarded at an equestrian center.

Camping

A 45-unit family campground has tables, drinking water, and modern restrooms with hot showers; group sites also available.

Picnicking

Picnic sites feature tables, barbecue grills, adjacent turf areas for games, and a children's playground.

Fishing and Boating

Two natural lakes are stocked with trout and catfish; licenses sold in the park. Trout derbies are scheduled frequently during the winter season. Rental pedal boats permit leisurely tours of park waterways.

How to Get There: Located in San Bernardino County, approximately 10 miles northwest of the City of San Bernardino. From LA, go east on I-10 to I-15 and turn north. Follow I-15 to the Devore off ramp (Sierra Ave.). Exit west and proceed a short distance to Devore Rd. Turn northeast onto Devore Rd. and proceed to Glen Helen Park; the main entrance is on the south (right) side of the road.

Open 7:30–dusk daily, year-round. Nominal vehicle admission fee.

For Additional Information:
Glen Helen Regional Park
2555 Devore Rd.
San Bernardino, CA 92407

714-880-2522

San Bernardino County Regional Parks Department
825 E. Third St.
San Bernardino, CA 92415

714-387-2594

17. Hamilton Preserve

This starkly beautiful wildlife sanctuary covers 40 acres of high desert country near the northern border of Angeles National Forest (described elsewhere). Shaped by two earthquake faults, the San Andreas to the north and the San Jacinto to the south, the landscape contains some striking geologic features. Cottonwoods and willows adorn the banks of Sandrock Creek, a seasonal stream that meanders through a steep canyon on the western half of the preserve. The walls of the canyon and some precipitous sandstone cliffs are dotted with small caves and crevices that are used as nesting sites by ravens, owls, hawks, and swifts. Many other species of birds find shelter in the piñon-juniper woodland that makes up the dominant plant community of the preserve. Also living in this remote area are gray foxes, raccoons, coyotes, rattlesnakes, scorpions, kangaroo rats, and a variety of lizards.

Visitor activities are limited to such passive recreation as hiking, nature study, and photography. A picnic area, restrooms, and drinking water are available at nearby Devil's Punchbowl County Regional Park (described elsewhere).

Hiking

In this wild and remote place, you may make your own way through the preserve. Visitors should avoid trampling the vegetation as much as possible and keep an eye out for rattlesnakes and scorpions. Climbing the cliffs is risky.

How to Get There: Located in east central Los Angeles County. From LA, go north on I-5 to CA 14 (Antelope Valley Fwy.), then go northeast on CA 14 to the Little Rock turnoff just beyond Vincent. Travel east on the turnoff (also known as Pearblossom Hwy. and, for part of the route, as CA 138) through Little Rock and Pearblossom. Just beyond Pearblossom, look for the Devil's Punchbowl County Regional Park sign, turn south on Co. Rd. N-6, and follow the signs to Devil's Punchbowl. N-6 first follows Longview Rd. (131st St.) south, then jogs east on Fort Tejon Rd., then turns south again on Longview Rd. (131st St.), and finally turns east on Tumbleweed Rd. (also known as Devil's Punchbowl Rd.). Tumbleweed Rd. eventually enters Angeles National Forest and ends a short distance later in Devil's Punchbowl County Regional Park. Approximately 100 yards before you enter Angeles National Forest, a dirt road leads east to some large sandstone cliffs. Follow this dirt road for about ½ a mile, past a gate, to the top of a bluff that overlooks the preserve; an old road then leads down to the preserve's southwest corner. Park along road.

Open daily, year-round, during daylight hours. Free.

For Additional Information:
The Nature Conservancy
Southern California Chapter Project Office
213 Stearns Wharf
Santa Barbara, CA 93101

805-962-9111

The Nature Conservancy
California Field Office
785 Market St.
San Francisco, CA 94103

415-777-0487

18. Harper Dry Lake

Irrigation on nearby farmlands has, in recent years, produced enough runoff to transform Harper Dry Lake into a marsh. Among the waterfowl and shore birds that visit here are the bald eagle and the Yuma clapper rail, both endangered species. The Bureau of Land Management, which administers this part of the Mojave Desert, plans to build a boardwalk and observation tower and to offer interpretive programs in the near future.

How to Get There: Located in west central San Bernardino County, northwest of Barstow; the lake is shown on the official California road map. From LA, go east on I-10 to I-15. Go north on I-15 to the CA 58 exit just past Barstow. Take CA 58 west for about 20 miles to Harper Lake Rd., and turn north. Harper Lake Rd. ends at Harper Dry Lake. Lockhart Rd. (a dirt road) leads east off of Harper Lake Rd., just before the latter road ends, to another part of the lake. Other dirt roads, some graded, skirt and cross the lake.

Open at all times. Free.

For Additional Information:
Desert Information Ctr.
Bureau of Land Management
831 Barstow Rd.
Barstow, CA 92311

619-256-8617

California Desert District Office
Bureau of Land Management
1695 Spruce St.
Riverside, CA 92507

714-351-6394

19. Los Angeles State and County Arboretum

Once part of a millionaire's 8,000-acre estate, the Los Angeles State and County Arboretum abounds with botanical life from all over the world, arranged by place of origin or period of history. Many of the more than 30,000 plants that grow on the arboretum's 127-

acre grounds were obtained through an international exchange program with 130 botanical gardens, including several in Russia and China.

One of the loveliest areas is a tangle of wild grapevines, bamboo, ginger, willows, orchids, bromeliads, and palm trees known as the Prehistoric and Jungle Garden. The cycads, redwoods, and sago palms found herein are among the most primitive plants on earth.

In a recent Texas-Florida-California face-off to determine which state contained the tallest palm tree, Texas and Florida came up with single specimens that measured 61 feet and 68 feet respectively. The LA Arboretum's Jungle Garden boasted more than two dozen palms that exceeded 75 feet in height and four that were nearly 150 feet tall.

Peacocks and guinea fowl roam the grounds, and a spring-fed lagoon lures many migratory waterfowl. More than 150 other species of birds may be seen here year-round.

Numerous paths meander through all this fragrant lushness, past waterfalls, streams, lily ponds, and various demonstration gardens, to a greenhouse where orchids always bloom. Also on the grounds are an herbarium, several historical buildings, a reference library, some picnic tables, and gift and coffee shops.

If it all seems familiar to you, it may be because the arboretum has served as the setting for many jungle movies. The television show *Fantasy Island* used Lasca Lagoon as a backdrop, and the leech-filled waters through which Humphrey Bogart pulled the *African Queen* are on these premises.

Just east of the arboretum, on land that was once part of the same estate, lies the Santa Anita Race Track. Its grounds are lavishly planted with flowers, including approximately one million special Santa Anita pansies that are in peak bloom during the thoroughbred racing season (December 26 to mid-April). On the day the season ends, gardeners dig up the plants and give them away on a first-come basis. Each racing season starts with a fresh crop.

How to Get There: From downtown LA, go east on I-10 to Baldwin Ave. and turn north. The arboretum is about 4½ miles north of I-10, on the west side of Baldwin Ave. opposite the Santa Anita Race Track. Parking on site.

Open 9–4:30 daily, year-round; closed December 25. Nominal admission fee; under 5 free. Open-air tram tours 12:15–3 Monday–Friday; 10:30–4 Saturday and Sunday; fare charged (free third Tuesday of each month).

For Additional Information:
Los Angeles State & County Arboretum
301 N. Baldwin Ave.
Arcadia, CA 91006

818-446-8251

20. Mojave Narrows Regional Park

This is a marvelous park, lush and serene, a place suspended in time. Broad meadows are cooled by clusters of cottonwood and willow trees in places and are open to the warmth of the sun elsewhere. More trees line the acres of waterways—ponds, creeks, two lakes—and a marsh filled with wildlife. On pasture land adjoining the park, cows graze near a silo.

The San Bernardino County Regional Parks Department, which administers this 840-acre park but leaves most of the landscaping to nature, describes it as Huck Finn country. Indeed it is.

Hiking

Miles of hiking trails lead through the woodlands; one scenic trail is especially designed for the handicapped.

Camping

A 100-unit campground with picnic tables, barbecue grills, and restrooms with hot showers is available year-round except Christmas Day.

Picnicking

Secluded and peaceful picnic areas offer tables and grills; drinking water and a playground also available.

Fishing and Boating

Horseshoe Lake, the larger of two park lakes, offers some of the finest bass and catfish angling in the area;

fishing licenses and bait available in the park. Rowboats, as well as pedal boats, may be rented at the
boathouse.

How to Get There: Located in southwestern San Ber-
nardino County, near Victorville. From LA, go east on
I-10 to I-15, and turn north. Follow I-15 to the Bear
Valley Cutoff, and turn east, proceeding to Ridge Crest
Rd. Turn north, and follow Ridge Crest to the park.
Look for signs.
    Open 7:30 A.M.–sunset daily. Nominal vehicle ad-
mission fee.

For Additional Information:
Mojave Narrows Regional Park
P.O. Box 361
Victorville, CA 92393

619-245-2226

San Bernardino County Regional Parks Department
825 E. Third St.
San Bernardino, CA 92415

714-387-2594

21. Pacific Crest National Scenic Trail

One of the most scenic and adventurous hiking trails
in America, the Pacific Crest Trail extends 2,600 miles
between our country's northern and southern boundaries. The trail, so named because it generally follows
the crest of mountain ranges along its route through
Washington, Oregon, and California, may also be used
by horseback riders.
    Within the radius covered by this book, the trail
enters the Sequoia, Angeles, and San Bernardino national forests and Mount San Jacinto State Park and
Wilderness (all described elsewhere), crosses Bureau
of Land Management land, and passes through some
private property. The varied terrain—mountains, forests, deserts—provides the opportunity to see a great
diversity of flora and fauna. Bands of bighorn sheep
are sometimes spotted in the high country, and on
rare occasions, the elusive cougar makes an appear-

ance. Spring, with its bounteous wildflowers, pleasant temperatures, and plentiful water, is the best time to explore the trail. There are several access points along the trail's route, and camping is permitted.

Before starting out, obtain a trail map and check conditions in the area in which you will be traveling. Portions of the trail pass through wilderness areas, and drinking water can be difficult to find. At this writing, a few segments of the trail are not yet completed.

How to Get There: Since the trail is extensive and there are many ways to get there, anyone interested should contact the information sources listed here and then decide where to enter the trail. At that time, directions may be obtained from any of these information sources.

For Additional Information:
Office of Information
Pacific Southwest Region
USDA—Forest Service
630 Sansome St.
San Francisco, CA 94111
415-556-0122

Pacific Crest Club
P.O. Box 1907
Santa Ana, CA 92702
(No phone—send self-addressed, stamped envelope)

Information Officer
Sequoia National Forest Headquarters
900 W. Grand Ave.
Porterville, CA 93257
209-784-1500

Angeles National Forest
701 N. Santa Anita Ave.
Arcadia, CA 91006
818-574-5200

San Bernardino National Forest
1824 S. Commercenter Circle
San Bernardino, CA 92408
714-383-5588

Bureau of Land Management
Bakersfield District Office
800 Truxtun Ave.
Bakersfield, CA 93301
805-861-4191

Mount San Jacinto State Park
P.O. Box 308
Idyllwild, CA 92349
714-659-2607

22. Rainbow Basin/Owl Canyon

The forces of erosion have been at work for centuries in Rainbow Basin, carving out the deep canyons, sculpting the bizarre rock formations, and revealing the richly colored rock layers that make this one of the most outstanding scenic areas in the Mojave Desert.

Formed some 10 to 30 million years ago, the 800-acre basin has also yielded some extraordinary fossils from the Miocene epoch. Many larger mammals of the period, including a prehistoric camel, left their tracks here, and the fossilized insects are considered the best-preserved specimens in the world. In recognition of its uniqueness, Rainbow Basin has been designated a National Natural Landmark.

Owl Canyon, just east of Rainbow Basin, has also yielded important geological and paleontological finds. The entire area is under the jurisdiction of the Bureau of Land Management.

Camping

More than thirty BLM campsites in Owl Canyon are available on a first-come basis; tents and RVs up to 24 feet. Picnic tables, grills, vault toilets, drinking water. Open all year; 14-day limit.

How to Get There: Located in west central San Bernardino County, northwest of Barstow. From LA, go east on I-10 to I-15, and go north on I-15 to the Barstow Rd. exit in Barstow. Go north on Barstow Rd. to Main St.; turn west onto Main St. and go to First Ave.; go north on First Ave. to Ft. Irwin Rd. Take Ft. Irwin

Rd. west and north for about 6 miles to Fossil Bed Rd.
Take Fossil Bed Rd. west for about 3 miles to Rainbow
Basin Rd., a 4-mile-long scenic loop on the north side
of the road. Approximately ½ mile north of Fossil Bed
Rd., a road leads east off of Rainbow Basin Rd. into
Owl Canyon. (Ft. Irwin Rd. is paved; all others are
graded dirt.)

Open at all times. Rainbow Basin is free; nominal
fee for campground.

For Additional Information:
Desert Information Ctr.
Bureau of Land Management
831 Barstow Rd.
Barstow, CA 92311

619-256-8617

California Desert District Office
Bureau of Land Management
1695 Spruce St.
Riverside, CA 92507

714-351-6394

23. Red Rock Canyon State Recreation Area

Particularly beautiful when touched by the low rays
of a rising or setting sun, the cliffs and palisades of
Red Rock Canyon range in color from stark white to
vivid red to dark chocolate brown. The array of hori-
zontally layered hues, exposed over the centuries by
erosion in an area of the Mojave Desert that remains
virtually undisturbed to this day, is both visually
striking and geologically significant. By studying the
rock formations and the wealth of fossil remains
found within this rugged, 4,000-acre park and the
nearby El Paso Mountains, scientists have been able
to reconstruct 500 million years of the natural history
of this part of California.

Rare and endangered plant species in the park include the Red Rock tarweed, Mojave fishhook cactus,
and spiny chorizanthe. After a wet winter, the area
boasts an amazingly diverse display of spring wildflowers. A variety of birds can also be seen here, but

because Red Rock Canyon lies along the north and south migration routes, many are only visitors. Hawks, roadrunners, horned larks, ravens, and, near the natural springs and water seeps, quail and chukar partridge may be sighted throughout the year. Also residing here, but rarely seen, are rattlesnakes, scorpions, tarantulas, desert tortoises, and the endangered Mojave ground squirrels. Complete flora and fauna lists are available at the park office.

Hiking

Several miles of primitive roads lead hikers throughout most of the park; some roads continue onto Bureau of Land Management land adjacent to the state recreation area. Hikers must make their own way, however, through the Hagen Canyon and Red Cliffs natural preserves, two particularly scenic and fragile areas in the heart of the park.

Camping

A primitive campground with fifty tent and trailer sites is located near park headquarters; tables, stoves, piped drinking water, pit toilets, disposal station. Reservations accepted, but not required. Open all year.

Picnicking

No formally developed picnic areas exist, but visitors may picnic in unoccupied campsites.

How to Get There: Located in southeast central Kern County. From LA, go north on I-5 to CA 14 (Antelope Valley Fwy.) and turn east. Follow CA 14 east and then north through the town of Mojave. The state recreation area lies on both sides of CA 14 about 25 miles northeast of Mojave; look for signs along the way.

Open daily, year-round, sunrise to sunset. Nominal vehicle admission fee.

For Additional Information:
Department of Parks & Recreation
State of California
High Desert Area
General William J. Fox Airfield
4555 West Avenue G
Lancaster, CA 93536

805-942-0662

Red Rock Canyon State Recreation Area
RRC Box 26
Cantil, CA 93519
(No phone)

24. Saddleback Butte State Park

Saddleback Butte, a granite mountaintop that inter-
rupts the flatness of the surrounding terrain, stands at
the western edge of the Mojave Desert. Near its base
is a forest of Joshua trees, not really trees at all but
unusual members of the lily family that can grow up
to 40 feet tall. It was to preserve both the butte and
the forest that this 2,875-acre park was created in
1960, and development has been kept to a minimum
to protect these natural features.

The desert tortoise lives here, as do the sidewinder
and Mojave rattlesnakes, chuckwalla, desert spiny
lizard, golden eagle, marsh hawk, raven, roadrunner,
and several species of owls. In spring, the park and
valley around it put on a wildflower extravaganza that
is unparalleled anywhere in southern California. Visitors will see desert paintbrush, little gold poppy,
dune primrose, Mojave sand verbena, and, except in
unusually dry years, the waxy white blossoms that
cluster at the tips of the Joshua tree's angular
branches.

A small Visitor Center, located at the main entrance, provides checklists of park birds, mammals,
reptiles, and plants.

Hiking

A trail that climbs up Saddleback Butte provides a
4-mile round trip. Next to the Visitor Center, a nature
trail follows a ½-mile-long loop.

Camping

A family campground containing fifty primitive sites
lies about one mile south of park headquarters; facilities include tables, stoves, pit toilets, drinking water.

Picnicking

There is one picnic area in the park. Its location on a
small ridge near the main entrance offers a view of

Saddleback Butte. Tables, char-wood stoves, pit toilets, drinking water available.

How to Get There: Located in Antelope Valley in northeastern Los Angeles County. From LA, go north on I-5 to CA 14 (Antelope Valley Fwy.). Take CA 14 east and then north to E. Ave. J (Co. Rd. N-5) in Lancaster. Turn east to park's main entrance on the south side of E. Ave. J (just east of the intersection of E. Ave. J and N. 170th St. East).

Open 24 hours daily, year-round. Nominal vehicle entry fee.

For Additional Information:
California Department of Parks & Recreation
High Desert Area Headquarters
4555 W. Ave. G
Lancaster, CA 93546

805-942-0662

25. San Andreas Fault

California is literally riddled with earthquake faults, and new ones are still being discovered, but it is the San Andreas Fault that is the longest and best known. It is also the most conspicuous rift of its kind in the world. Along its path from the Mexican border to Mendocino County north of San Francisco, the San Andreas Fault has created an almost continuous chain of highly visible topographic features.

Perhaps the best area in which to view the fault's features is the Carrizo Plain, a 50-mile-long, 6-mile-wide stretch of desolate and arid land in southeastern San Luis Obispo County. Here geologists discovered more than 125 small streams whose channels had been offset from 20 to 50 feet each by the right lateral slip that characterizes the entire San Andreas Fault (i.e., if you stand on either side of the fault and look across it, the landscape on the other side appears to have moved to the right). Displaced by the Fort Tejon earthquake of 1857, a violent shudder that created a 200-mile-long fracture on the surface of the earth and shoved the west side of the San Andreas Fault northward as much as 30 feet, these streams turn sharply as they cross the fault line. Other easily discernible features sculpted by the restless fault include steep cliffs known as scarps and a series of sag ponds (depressions in the earth that fill with water because they have no drainage outlet). Since low light and long shadows help delineate the fault line, you should visit the Carrizo Plain during early morning or late afternoon hours.

Visitors who come to the plain during winter months may also enjoy an outstanding wildlife spectacle. From late November to May, when rains fill the summer-parched basin of Soda Lake, some 6,500 lesser sandhill cranes, several species of ducks, golden and bald eagles, red-tailed hawks, and prairie falcons congregate in the area.

Soda Lake is part of an ecological preserve that covers 2,960 acres on Bureau of Land Management land. Protected by a management agreement between BLM and The Nature Conservancy, the preserve is the core of a TNC project that will eventually insure protection for 200,000 acres of the Carrizo Plain. (For updated information, contact TNC at the address given at the end of this entry.)

Just southwest of Palmdale, the workings of the San Andreas Fault are vividly displayed in a highway cut that borders CA 14. The torturous buckling of rock formations seen on the rock wall were caused by tectonic compression. A nearby plaque depicts the location of the fault line and describes some of the features associated with it.

The rocks at Devil's Punchbowl County Regional Park (described elsewhere), a few miles southeast of Pearblossom, and the rocks seen in the Cajon Beds, which lie approximately 25 miles southeast of Devil's Punchbowl on the opposite side of the fault line, are believed to have once been part of the same rock formation, separated over the years by horizontal fault movements.

Nearly all of the 150 or so palm oases in the southwestern United States and northern Mexico occur along fault lines, and some of the most beautiful lie along the San Andreas. The fault is responsible for releasing the groundwater that nurtures the verdant growth in these oases. Although it lies slightly beyond the 100-mile radius covered by this book, Thousand

Palms Oasis east of Palm Springs is one of the largest and most impressive of the San Andreas oases. It lies in the heart of The Nature Conservancy's Coachella Valley Preserve.

Estimated to be 100 million years old, the San Andreas Fault is 700 miles long within California and varies in width from about 100 yards to a mile or more in the central and northern parts of the state. South of the San Gorgonio Pass (a deep cleft between San Jacinto and San Gorgonio mountains, the two highest peaks in Southern California), the San Andreas is made up of several parallel branches whose combined width nearly equals the width of the state.

No one, however, has to worry about the often repeated prediction that California will slide into the sea. The Pacific Ocean is only two miles deep in this part of the world, and California is 20 to 30 miles thick.

If you plan to do much exploring along the San Andreas, you should so some advance research to acquaint yourself with the fault's exact path and the characteristics of its surface features. One source is a book called *Earthquake Country: How, Why and Where Earthquakes Strike in California* (Lane Publishing Co., 1964). Although now out of print, it's available at many libraries. Most bookstores in California stock maps of the state's known earthquake faults, and the California Division of Mines & Geology publishes a definitive fault map that also shows the locations of volcanoes, thermal springs, and thermal wells (see addresses at the end of this entry).

How to Get There: The San Andreas Fault runs in a generally northwest-southeast direction from the Mexican border to Point Arena in Mendocino County. Once you have learned to recognize its basic features, you can follow the fault for miles along public roads. Directions for reaching the places specifically mentioned in this entry follow:

To reach the Carrizo Plain from LA, go north on I-5 to CA 58 in Kern County. Turn west and follow CA 58 approximately 44 miles to the California Valley turnoff road. Go south on the turnoff road, through the town of California Valley, for about 10 miles to a small parking lot on the east side of the road next to a metal telephone company building. A short, self-guiding trail leads from the parking area to Soda Lake. From the parking lot, the turnoff road (also known as Soda Lake Rd.) continues south another 35 miles to CA 33/166. Soda Lake Rd.—partially paved, partially gravel and dirt—is the main road through the Carrizo Plain, but there are several other dirt roads as well. Be sure you have a good area map and plenty of gas and water before starting out. The Carrizo Plain is desolate and undeveloped.

To view the highway cut near Palmdale, take I-5 north from LA to CA 14 (Antelope Valley Fwy.) and turn northeast. The highway cut is visible from CA 14 just southwest of Palmdale. To learn more about this and other fault features in the area, stop at the pullout located along the freeway just south of the Avenue S off ramp and read the plaque that has been erected there.

Directions for reaching Devil's Punchbowl County Regional Park, which lies about 25 miles southeast of Palmdale at the northern edge of the Angeles National Forest, are given elsewhere as part of that park's description. To reach the Cajon Beds from Palmdale, go east on CA 138 for about 48 miles. The tilted rocks of the Cajon Beds—apricot-tinted sandstone outcroppings also known as the Rock Candy Mountains and Mormon Rocks—can be seen along both sides of CA 138 near the Mormon Rocks Ranger Station in the San Bernardino National Forest.

To reach Thousand Palms Oasis from LA, go east on I-10 to the Thousand Palms exit (Ramon Rd.) in Riverside County. Continue east on Ramon Rd., through the town of Thousand Palms, to Thousand Palms Canyon Rd. and turn north. Proceed north for about 1½ miles; Thousand Palms Oasis lies on the west side of Thousand Palms Canyon Rd. On the east side of the road, opposite the oasis, is another interesting area to explore—Indio Palms County Park, 1,690 acres of currently undeveloped land that lies atop the San Andreas Fault and is available for hiking and nature study. To reach the park entrance, take Thousand Palms Canyon Rd. south to Ramon Rd., go east for approximately 1¾ miles (Ramon Rd. becomes Washington St. along the way), and turn left into the park.

For Additional Information:
California Department of Conservation
Division of Mines & Geology
107 S. Broadway St.
Los Angeles, CA 90012

213-620-3560

California Department of Conservation
Division of Mines & Geology
380 Civic Dr.
Pleasant Hill, CA 94523

415-646-5922

State Geologist
California Department of Conservation
Division of Mines & Geology
660 Bercut Dr.
Sacramento, CA 95814

916-445-5716

The Nature Conservancy
California Field Office
785 Market St.
San Francisco, CA 94103

415-777-0487

26. San Bernardino National Forest

Sprawling over more than half a million acres of the most rugged territory east of Los Angeles is the San Bernardino National Forest. Much of it is strikingly scenic, ranging from lowland desert where Joshua trees grow to peaks capped with snow most of the year. It is laced with earthquake fault areas, including the San Andreas (described elsewhere), which crosses California from the Salton Sea to San Francisco Bay. It would be difficult to find a more diverse national forest within the entire nation, or one with greater variety in terrain, flora, and fauna.

At least twenty-five species of plant life within the forest are listed as threatened; several of them show up on the endangered plant list compiled by the U.S. Fish & Wildlife Service. A number of animals living here are either threatened with imminent extinction or are on the endangered species list, including the desert bighorn sheep, bald eagle, peregrine falcon, and golden eagle.

Located just an hour east of Los Angeles, the San Bernardino is primarily mountain country. For years the movie companies of Hollywood have searched out its primeval beauty for shooting westerns. There are gentle flatlands and rolling hills, sheer escarpments and rock-ribbed peaks, hot slopes smothered in thorny chapparal, cool subalpine forests of Douglas fir and ponderosa pine. In the desert valleys, it almost never snows, but in the high country snowbanks linger eight months of the year.

Three distinct mountain ranges traverse the San Bernardino—the San Jacintos in the south, a northern extension of the Peninsular Range jutting northward from Mexico; the San Bernardinos; and the San Gabriels. San Gorgonio Peak in the San Bernardino Mountains is the highest point (11,502 feet) in southern California, but there are more than half a dozen peaks rising up to 10,000 feet. San Gorgonio Peak stands in about the center of the San Gorgonio Wilderness, one of five separate wilderness areas within the national forest. The others are Cucamonga, San Jacinto, Santa Rosa, and Sheep Mountain.

Most popular is the San Gorgonio, the largest wilderness area in southern California. It's a high wilderness; the boundary line is drawn at 7,000 feet elevation, and there are nine peaks ranging above 10,000 feet. It also includes two glacier-carved cirque lakes, good examples of arctic-alpine forest life, and glacially deposited moraines, and it is the headwaters for two rivers—the Santa Ana and the Whitewater. A herd of endangered Nelson bighorn sheep roams free here.

The San Jacinto Wilderness, located on the south side of Banning Pass, is the only wilderness area in the nation, perhaps the entire world, where visitors can take a cable car to its door. The aerial tramway at Palm Springs transports people from the desert valley far below to the rim of the San Jacinto Range, immediately putting them in touch with a true wilderness experience.

The San Jacinto Wilderness and the adjoining Mount San Jacinto Wilderness State Park together encompass most of the San Jacinto Mountain Range. The entire northern portion and the Andreas and Murray desert canyons of the southern portion include some of the steepest, most rugged terrain in the entire nation. The northern escarpment plunges dramatically in sheer cliffs and ridges to Banning Pass (9,000 feet in four miles). Snow Creek and its tributaries have carved deep canyons in the escarpment face, affording excellent cross-country skiing in winter and hiking and climbing in summer. Awesome views of the surrounding desert valleys can be enjoyed from these mountains.

The southern portion is a well-watered plateau with numerous stream-fed mountain meadows and a portion of the San Jacinto ridgetop known as the Desert Divide. The San Jacinto Wilderness also includes one of the most outstanding landmarks of the southern California landscape—Lily (Tahquitz) Rock, a most popular challenge for rock climbers.

More than 50 percent of the San Bernardino National Forest is characterized by mountain slope terrain, some of it quite steep. On the southern faces of the east-west ranges, the mountains feature deep canyons and steep slopes that rise to broad, flat ridges with occasional high peaks. To the north and east they slope more gradually down to the Mojave Desert.

Cutting across the forest diagonally from Cajon Pass on the northwest boundary southeastward along the base of the San Bernardino Mountains to Banning Pass is the San Andreas Fault, the longest earthquake fault zone in the entire Northern Hemisphere and perhaps in the world. Both it and the neighboring San Jacinto Fault are also among the most active faults in this hemisphere; measureable earthquakes and tremors are an almost daily occurrence, although many visitors do not notice them. Both faults are capable of major violent activity at any time, however. Hikers particularly should be aware that a study done for the Division of Dam Safety in California states that an earthquake of magnitude 8 on the Richter scale in the vicinity of privately owned Great Bear Lake dam could create enough force to destroy the dam, which in turn would permit onrush flooding of a great area of the national forest.

One of the reasons for earthquake activity in the area is that, geologically, these mountains are young. Nonetheless, erosion has already removed much of the sediment and formations of shale, sandstone, and limestone, leaving impressive outcrops of granite rock in many places. The Mormon Rocks just off I-15 shortly after it divides from I-10 heading east are an excellent example. Because slopes of the mountains are steep, much of the surface remains unstable and subject to movement.

No volcanic activity has been recorded within the national forest, but there has been ash fallout from caldera in Long Valley in Mono County, some 150 miles to the north, and from the volcanic area near Amboy, 50 miles to the northeast.

Dispersed throughout the forest are riparian areas like desert oases, rich in plant and animal life. In the lower elevations, water is often scarce and the riparian areas are surprisingly dense and diverse. Springs provide most of that water, and much that lives in the desert is drawn to these areas.

In addition, there are sparkling mountain lakes— Big Bear, Arrowhead, Silverwood, and Hemet are the major ones—boggy meadows, quiet brooks, and, in higher elevations, rushing streams. In some cases, barrel cactus and Joshua trees, both notably desert plants, are found close by Jeffrey pines and incense cedars. Piñons, junipers, and sagebrush cover mid-elevation desert slopes while conifer and oak forests dominate altitudes of over 6,000 feet. Ancient, 2,000-year-old limber pines are found sporadically in the San Gorgonio Wilderness Area.

Wild burros, bobcats, raccoons, owls, ring-tailed cats, eagles, coyotes, mountain lions, black bears, and two species of desert bighorn sheep roam the area, and, not so long ago, there were occasional sightings of the rare California condor, now extinct in the wild. Mule deer are plentiful.

In Holcomb Valley gold is still there to this day. Old prospectors claim there is a mother lode vein there, and in the 1860s the magic of riches caused a major gold rush in this area. A trail leads past and through the ruins and scratchings of that era.

Numerous archaeological discoveries over the years show at least three Indian cultures lived in this area of the forest—the Serrano, Cahuilla, and Luiseño. Probably all three tribes were here when the first Europeans moved into the area in the eighteenth century. Many of the hot springs, mountains, and rock formations were named by these Indians; some of them were sacred. Tahquitz Peak in the San Jacintos, for instance, which attracts rock climbers today, was the home of the legendary evil god Tahquitz, who, remains very real to the Cahuilla and Serrano peoples still living in the area.

Hiking

Although there are areas for off-road vehicle use in some parts of the forest, a primary and more desirable recreation opportunity here is hiking. More than a dozen major trails traverse the forest, including more than 40 miles of the transcontinental Pacific Crest National Scenic Trail, which wends its way up the crown of the Sierra Nevada Mountains to the Canadian border. In all, there are more than 510 miles of trail within the national forest, and more than 80 percent of them are classified as rugged and difficult. Yet some simple, less challenging trails exist, such as Seeley Creek, which only extends one mile and is classified as easy. Hikers are urged to beware of possible hazards such as falling trees, steep drop-offs, rattlesnakes, particularly in shaded areas or near water, and swift streams. The U.S. Forest Service provides a free directory of hiking trails. Send a stamped self-addressed envelope (see address at the end of this entry). Maps are available for $1.

Fishing

In addition to such major lakes as Big Bear, Silverwood, Hemet, and Arrowhead, there are some 80 miles of trout streams in the forest. Native rainbow trout provide the finest fishing experience, but reaching many of these locations requires backpacking and/or hiking along rugged trails. Largemouth bass, bream, catfish, and various trout are found in the lakes.

Camping

Camping is possible throughout the national forest. Some private campgrounds offer first-class facilities with full hookups for water, electricity, and sewage. U.S. Forest Service campgrounds vary in facilities offered and fees charged. Remote backcountry sites are free. For further campground information, contact the San Bernardino National Forest headquarters. Many campgrounds are open year-round; others in the higher country are closed during winter.

Picnicking

Picnic facilities are provided at many of the campground sites. Check with the Forest Service headquarters for details and maps showing exact locations.

For Additional Information:
U.S. Forest Service
San Bernardino National Forest
1824 S. Commercenter Circle
San Bernardino, CA 92408

714-383-5588

27. San Dimas Canyon Park

Although small, this 138-acre park maintains the aura of a natural woodland. Huge oak trees dominate the landscape and crowd close to the stream that flows through the northern part of the park. Visitors can learn about the ecology of the area at the park's nature center and wildlife zoo.

Picnicking

The sprawling, oak-shaded picnic area is one of the most popular in eastern Los Angeles County; grills are provided. Open play fields, as well as shuffleboard and horseshoe courts, are nearby.

How to Get There: Located in southeastern Los Angeles County. From LA, go east on I-10 to I-210, and take I-210 north to CA 30. Go east on CA 30 to San Dimas Ave., then north on San Dimas to Foothill Blvd., east on Foothill Blvd. to San Dimas Canyon Rd., and north on San Dimas Canyon Rd. to Sycamore Canyon Rd. Continue north on Sycamore Canyon Rd. into the park.

Park open during daylight hours; nature center open 9–5 Saturday–Thursday. Both free.

For Additional Information:
San Dimas Canyon Park Nature Center
1512 N. Sycamore Canyon Rd.
San Dimas, CA 91773

714-599-7512

County of Los Angeles
Department of Parks & Recreation
433 S. Vermont Ave.
Los Angeles, CA 90020

213-738-2961

28. Solar One

From a distance, when the sun beats down, it looks
as if a jumble of brilliant diamonds has been strewn
across the desert floor. As you draw nearer, you realize that the "jewels" are actually giant mirrors—1,818
of them, programmed by computer to follow the arc
of the sun across the sky and focus the sun's rays on
a stainless steel cylinder atop a 300-foot-tall tower.
Solar One, as the project is called, is the country's
first commercial solar-thermal plant.

Built at a cost of $140 million to test the technolog-
ical and economical feasibility of solar energy, Solar
One has been in operation since January 1982. No
longer open to visitors but you can drive past. Spectacular view.

How to Get There: Located east of Barstow in San
Bernardino County. From LA, take I-10 east to I-15,
then take I-15 north. Near Barstow, pick up I-40 and
go southeast to the Daggett exit. Go north on this exit
road to National Trails Rd. and turn east. Go about 3
miles; Solar One lies on the north side of National
Trails Rd. You can see as much from the road as you
would inside.

For Additional Information:
Desert Information Ctr.
831 Barstow Rd.
Barstow, CA 92311

619-256-8617

29. Vasquez Rocks County Park

Vasquez Rocks County Park, an eerie fantasyland of
sand and stone, contains some of the state's most
noted geological wonders. The stark, lonely landscape is studded with giant sandstone slabs, left

wildly tilted by long-ago movements of the restless San Andreas Fault (described elsewhere). Some of the rocks soar hundreds of feet above the desert floor, creating an irresistible temptation for rock climbers of all ages. Junipers, yuccas, scrub oaks, and creosote bushes populate the mesa from which the rocks rise, and a seasonal stream meanders through the area.

A recent acquisition of the Los Angeles County park system, this 745-acre wilderness is managed primarily as a natural area. An interpretive center, planned for the near future, will feature exhibits on both the natural and archaeological riches of the park. Until then, the area will be under the jurisdiction of the supervisor at Placerita Canyon State and County Park (described elsewhere).

Hiking and Horseback Riding

There is no formal trail system, but visitors on foot or horseback may explore any part of the park, including caves and canyons that once made ideal hideouts for nineteenth-century bandits.

Picnicking

A picnic area and comfort stations are located near the entrance.

How to Get There: Located in northernmost Los Angeles County about 8 miles west of Acton. From LA, go north on I-5 to CA 14 (Antelope Valley Fwy.), turn northeast, and follow CA 14 about 14 miles to Agua Dulce Canyon Rd. Turn north (left) onto Agua Dulce Rd. and proceed to Escondido Canyon Rd. Turn east (right) and continue a short distance to the park on the right (south) side of the road. There are several park signs along the way, including one on CA 14.

Open 8 A.M.–sundown daily, year-round. Free.

For Additional Information:
Vasquez Rocks County Park
10700 W. Escondido Rd.
Saugus, CA 91350

805-268-0840

Placerita Canyon Nature Center
19152 W. Placerita Canyon Rd.
Newhall, CA 91321

805-259-7721

County of Los Angeles
Department of Parks & Recreation
433 S. Vermont Ave.
Los Angeles, CA 90020

213-738-2961

30. Whittier Narrows Dam Recreation Area

The easternmost part of this 1,092-acre park has been set aside for nature study. Situated on 277 acres along the San Gabriel River, the natural area offers a nature center, a native plant nursery, several small lakes that lure myriads of migratory birds, and a raptor sanctuary. More than 150 species of plants and animals thrive within its confines.

Facilities elsewhere in the recreation area include ball diamonds, a soccer field, a skeet and trap shooting area, and archery and pistol ranges.

Hiking, Bicycling, and Horseback Riding

The Los Angeles County Department of Parks and Recreation has established one of the most extensive urban trail systems in the country—currently consisting of more than 225 miles—and Whittier Narrows Dam Recreation Area is the hub of that system. The Rio Hondo River and San Gabriel River trails, used by hikers, bicyclists, and equestrians, run through the recreation area in a north/south direction and connect with other trails in Los Angeles County. The Skyline and San Jose trails for hikers and equestrians begin in Whittier Narrows and extend eastward beyond the recreation area's boundary. Whittier Narrows Bikeway is a 3½-mile-long path that lies completely within the park. Five miles of nature trails wind through the natural area.

Picnicking

Several picnic areas with grills are scattered throughout the park; children's play areas are nearby. Groceries and snacks may be purchased in the park daily June through August and on weekends September through May.

Fishing and Boating

Legg Lake, a series of three connected pools, is stocked with bass, catfish, and trout. Rowboats and fishing tackle may be rented at a park concession; bait and ice also available. Lake open all year; concession open daily June through August and weekends September through May.

How to Get There: Located in south central Los Angeles County. From downtown LA, take the Pomona Fwy. (CA 60) east to Durfee Ave. and turn southwest. Proceed to the Whittier Narrows Nature Center on the east (left) side of the road. Parking on site.

Park open daily during daylight hours. Free, but some use fees may be charged in summer. Nature Center open 9–5 daily; closed July 4, Thanksgiving, December 25. Free.

For Additional Information:
Whittier Narrows Nature Center
1000 N. Durfee Ave.
South El Monte, CA 91733

818-444-1872

III

South by
Southeast

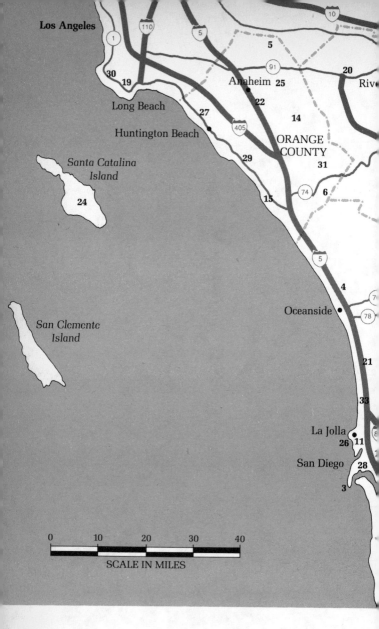

III: South by Southeast

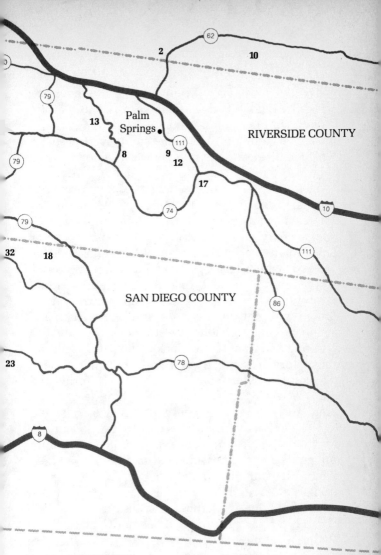

*Not shown on map. See text for description of location.

1. Balboa Park

One of the most magnificent urban parks anywere, 1,158-acre Balboa Park in San Diego is a mix of untouched wild lands and manicured grounds. It is also home to a variety of museums, sports facilities, theaters, botanical gardens, and the world-renowned San Diego Zoo.

Noted for its work in breeding rare and endangered animals, the zoo was the birthplace in 1983 of the first California condor successfully born in captivity. Only about twenty of these critically endangered birds were known to exist in the wild at that time. The 128-acre zoo, which features some 5,000 animals representing more than 1,600 species displayed in natural surroundings, is also a lush subtropical garden planted with unusual trees and shrubs. Elephant and camel rides are available on weekends.

Among other park attractions is the San Diego Natural History Museum, a showcase for the flora, fauna, and geological phenomena of southern California and Baja. Nearby is an area known as Florida Canyon, where gray fox, coyote, and gopher snakes live, and sightings of California quail, red-tailed hawk, and Anna's hummingbird are common. You may pick up a trail guide at the museum and explore the ¾-mile system on your own or take a free guided tour on Sundays at 2 P.M.

Elsewhere, the wilderness of space may be probed at the Fleet Space Theater and Science Center, where tilted seats and a huge hemispherical screen that virtually surrounds you create the feeling that you are in the movie. The Botanical Building contains more than 500 plant species, including an outstanding fern collection. Nearby, pink water lilies adorn the tranquil surface of a reflecting pool. There are several outdoor gardens, among them a rose garden, desert garden, sculpture garden, and a formal garden inspired by the gardens of the former Alcázar Castle in Seville, Spain. Just west of the Organ Pavilion (where free concerts are given periodically on an outdoor organ), you may descend a stairway into a wild arboretum of palm trees known as Palm Canyon.

There are miles of walkways to follow in the park, wooded areas to roam, and a dazzling array of such recreational facilities as a bowling green, archery field, tennis center, swimming pool, casting pool, roller skating area, a special play area for handicapped children, jogging paths, and golf courses. You may also ride a merry-go-round and a miniature railroad or take a tour of the park in a horse-drawn carriage.

Also located here are the Museum of San Diego History, Edison Centre for the Performing Arts, Balboa Art Conservation Center, Museum of Photographic Arts, Timken Art Gallery, San Diego Museum of Art, San Diego Art Institute, Aerospace Museum and International Aerospace Hall of Fame, Model Railroad Museum, Museum of Man, noted for its American Indian artifacts, House of Pacific Relations, a village of fifteen cottages where some twenty nations offer art and cultural exhibits, and the Hall of Champions, a tribute to local sports heroes.

Picnicking

Several picnic areas are located throughout the park —some in wooded groves, some in open fields, some with garden views. Food may be purchased at a concession stand near the center of the park; there are also restaurants within the park.

How to Get There: Balboa Park is located within the San Diego city limits, just northeast of the city's business district. From LA, take I-5 south to the Park Blvd. exit in San Diego. Take Park Blvd. north into the park. Look for Balboa Park signs along the way. Once in the park, look for signs directing you to the park information center in the House of Hospitality.

Park grounds open at all times. Free. Zoo open daily, year-round; 8:30–6 mid-June through Labor Day, 9–5 March to mid-June and after Labor Day–October, 9–4 November–February. Admission charged, free first Tuesday of each month. Museum of Natural History open daily, year-round, except Thanksgiving, Christmas, January 1; 10–5 mid-June to mid-September, 10–4:30 rest of year. Admission charged. Botanical Building open year-round, 10–4 Saturday–Thursday, except major holidays. Free. Fleet Space Theater presents several shows daily, year-round (phone for schedule). Admission charge (Science Center free with admission to Space Theater show). All other museums and facilities, except the swimming pool, are open year-round, but hours and days vary. Some charge admission.

For Additional Information:
Balboa Park Manager
Management Center
Balboa Park
San Diego, CA 92101

619-239-0512

(San Diego Zoo)

619-234-3153

(Natural History Museum)

619-232-3821

(Fleet Space Theater and Science Center)

619-238-1233

2. Big Morongo Canyon Preserve

Big Morongo Canyon Preserve near Palm Springs is nationally famous among naturalists, particularly bird watchers. More than 200 species of birds nest here, and several, including the vermilion flycatcher and Bell's vireo, are rare. Coyote and desert bighorn sheep roam the foothills of the San Bernardino Mountains.

Part of the preserve, fed by freshwater springs, is a cool green oasis in the midst of the desert that surrounds it. The creek that flows through Big Morongo Canyon is edged by lush foliage and graceful cottonwood trees that reach a height of 60 to 90 feet.

Because the preserve's 3,900 acres encompass parts of both the Mojave and Sonaran deserts, an unusual mix of plants in more than 150 varieties occurs here. Geologists will be interested in some ancient rocks on the preserve. Dated as nearly 2 billion years old, they are some of the oldest in California.

Hiking

More than 6 miles of trails lead throughout the preserve. They begin at the parking lot, enter the riparian forest, and extend the length of Big Morongo Canyon. Although rarely seen, rattlesnakes, scorpions, and black widow spiders live on the preserve, so be aware of your surroundings.

Picnicking

Although no picnic tables are available at the preserve itself, you'll find a picnic area and recreational facilities at adjacent Covington Park; restrooms and drinking water provided at both preserve and park.

How to Get There: From LA, drive east on I-10 to CA 62 (29 Palms Hwy.). Turn north on CA 62 and proceed approximately 9½ miles to East Dr. on the east side of the road, where you'll see a sign for Covington Park. Turn right, go 300 yards to the preserve entrance on your left. Parking on site. To reach Covington Park, continue past the preserve entrance a short distance, staying on East Dr., and turn left into park. Parking on site.

Preserve open daily, year-round, sunrise to sunset. Covington Park grounds open 6 A.M.–P.M. Both free.

For Additional Information:
Preserve Manager
Big Morongo Canyon Preserve
P.O. Box 780
Morongo Valley, CA 92256

619-363-7190

The Nature Conservancy
Southern California Chapter Project Office
213 Stearns Wharf
Santa Barbara, CA 93101

805-962-9111

The Nature Conservancy
California Field Office
785 Market St.
San Francisco, CA 94105

415-777-0487

3. Cabrillo National Monument

On the ocean side of the Point Loma peninsula, within the 144-acre Cabrillo National Monument, are some of the finest tide pools along the entire southern

California coast. Baby octopus, starfish, crabs, anemones, and sea hares are just a few of the creatures that live in this intermediary zone between land and sea —interesting any time, but best explored during the low tides of fall, winter, and spring.

From the restored lantern room in an old lighthouse, built in 1855 on a crest of land more than 420 feet above sea level, there are sweeping views of San Diego and its harbor, the mountains of Baja California a hundred miles to the south, and the La Jolla palisades to the north. (The *Encyclopaedia Britannica* has described this as one of the three most beautiful marine panoramas in the world.) An overlook about 100 yards south of the lighthouse is one of the best spots in the state from which to watch the annual gray whale migration. Each December through February, you can watch hundreds of spouting whales pass by on their journey from the Arctic to Baja (see Whale Migration). It's not uncommon to see seventy to eighty whales a day in mid-January.

Hiking

A nature trail provides a 2-mile round-trip hike through a mixture of desert and coastal vegetation in the eastern part of the monument. Also visible from the trail are the remnants of a coastal artillery system that defended San Diego Harbor during World Wars I and II. (Cabrillo National Monument is surrounded by military reservations.) The trail is open 9–4 daily.

How to Get There: Located within the city limits of San Diego. From LA, take I-5 south to San Diego and look for the Rosecrans St. (CA 209) exit. Follow Rosecrans St. southwest to Cañon St. and turn right. When Cañon St. ends at Catalina Blvd., turn left and proceed on Catalina Blvd. through the Naval Ocean System Center gates to the national monument at the end of the point. The Visitor Center distributes free literature about the park's features. Parking on site.

Open 9–5:15 daily, year-round. Free.

For Additional Information:
Cabrillo National Monument
P.O. Box 6670
San Diego, CA 92106
619-293-5450

4. Camp Pendleton Marine Base

Camp Pendleton, covering approximately 125,000 acres, borders the Pacific Ocean just north of Oceanside. In addition to being the largest Marine Corps base in the country, it is a major ecological preserve. Many species of wildlife make their homes here, lured by the chaparral-covered hills, mountains, canyons, marshlands, ponds, lakes, and seventeen miles of some of the finest shoreline in California.

The endangered California least tern made a dramatic comeback at Pendleton in the early 1970s, when in a single year the population grew from only thirty-eight birds to more than 600—three fourths of the total world population at the time. Watched over by protective Marines, the birds now nest undisturbed in the beach areas.

The camp's deer herd, carefully managed, numbers about 2,500 animals, and the wetlands attract more than twenty kinds of waterfowl.

Visitors may follow a self-guiding tour route that includes historic buildings, a museum, and views of the varied terrain. All wildlife habitats are stringently protected.

Camping

Year-round camping for self-contained RVs only is permitted at Las Pulgas Beach on Camp Pendleton. Access to the beach is controlled, and campers are chosen by a lottery. Applications for permits must be received at Camp Pendleton during the month of November; send two self-addressed stamped postcards, along with the names of all campers. Drawings take place the first week in December, at which time 1,000 applications are selected for the first period (February 1 through July 31) and another 1,000 applications for the second period (August 1 through January 31).

Fishing

Spotfin and yellowfin croakers and corbina await surf fishermen at Las Pulgas Beach. Anglers must apply for beach access permits in the same manner as campers.

How to Get There: Located in the northwest corner of San Diego County, just north of Oceanside. From

LA, go south on I-5. I-5 runs through Camp Pendleton near the ocean, paralleling the camp's beaches. Along the way, you will pass the Las Flores Viewpoint (where you may pull off for a view of the beach and adjacent bluffs) and the Aliso Creek Roadside Rest (picnic tables and a map showing local points of interest). After crossing the Santa Margarita River, look for a Camp Pendleton exit sign; the main entrance gate is located on Harbor Dr./Vandergrift Blvd. near the camp's southern boundary and just east of I-5.

Open 8–4 daily, year-round. Visitor pass and self-guided tour brochure are free; driver's license, vehicle registration, and verification of auto insurance are required to enter. Fee for camping and fishing permits.

For Additional Information:
Director, Natural Resources Office
Marine Corps Base
Camp Pendleton, CA 92055

619-725-6288 (General and Camping/fishing information)

5. Carbon Canyon Regional Park

Among the rolling foothills of the Chino Hill Range in northernmost Orange County is 124-acre Carbon Canyon Regional Park. Noted primarily for its 10-acre grove of coastal redwoods, a species rarely seen this far south, the park is also home to many other interesting trees. Pepper trees, sycamores, eucalyptus, and Canary Island pines dot the hills and perch on the banks of Carbon Canyon Creek, which runs through the length of the park.

The park also offers such recreational facilities as softball diamonds, a volleyball court, tennis courts, and a 4-acre fishing lake.

Hiking, Bicycling, and Horseback Riding

Hikers and equestrians share a 2-mile trail that leads to the redwood grove; bring your own horse. A 1½-mile bicycling trail is also available.

Picnicking

Picnic areas with covered ramadas and braziers are provided. Restrooms and children's playgrounds are nearby.

How to Get There: Located in the city of Brea. From LA, take I-10 east to CA 19; take CA 19 south to CA 60; proceed east on CA 60 to CA 57; go south on CA 57 to CA 90 (Imperial Hwy.) in Brea. Turn east on CA 90 and go to Valencia Ave. Go north on Valencia Ave., which swerves to the east and becomes Carbon Canyon Rd. The park lies on the south (right) side of Carbon Canyon Rd. Parking on site.

Open daily, year-round, 7 A.M.–10 P.M. April–September, 7 A.M.–sunset rest of year. Nominal vehicle admission fee.

For Additional Information:
Carbon Canyon Regional Park
4442 Carbon Canyon Rd.
Brea, CA 92621

714-996-5252

Environmental Management Agency
10852 Douglas Rd.
Anaheim, CA 92806

714-567-6206

6. Caspars Wilderness Park

Nestled among the foothills and sandstone canyons of the western Santa Ana Mountains is Caspars Wilderness Park—5,500 acres of fertile valleys, groves of coastal live oak, California sycamore, and, in the spring, multitudes of wildflowers. Formerly known as the Starr Viejo Regional Park, Caspars Park is managed primarily as a natural area, with development kept to a minimum. A guidebook, available for a small fee at the park office, describes the park's history, native plants, and wildlife.

Caspars Park is a facility of the Orange County Environmental Management Agency. It adjoins both the Cleveland National Forest and the Starr Ranch Audubon Sanctuary (both described elsewhere), which offer additional wilderness to explore.

Hiking and Horseback Riding

More than 18 miles of equestrian, hiking, and nature trails run throughout the park; bring your own horse. An illustrated booklet that describes many of the self-guiding trails is available for a nominal price at the park office.

Camping

Some eighty tent and RV campsites occupy 48 shady acres within the park; no hookups. Also hike-in campsites for backpackers, as well as a special equestrian campground equipped with hitching rails and corrals that can accommodate thirty vehicle/horse trailer combinations.

Picnicking

Family and group picnic areas contain tables and charcoal-burning grills. Hitching rails and corrals are available at equestrian picnic areas.

How to Get There: Located in southeast Orange County. From LA, take I-5 south to the Ortega Hwy. (CA 74) exit at San Juan Capistrano. Turn inland and follow the Ortega Hwy. east and north for approximately 7½ miles to the park entrance on the west side of the road at 33401 Ortega Hwy. Parking on site.

Open 7 A.M.–sunset daily, year-round. Nominal vehicle admission fee.

For Additional Information:
Caspars Wilderness Park
33401 Ortega Hwy.
San Juan Capistrano, CA 92675

714-831-2174

Orange County Environmental Management Agency
Open Space–Recreation Office
10852 Douglas Rd.
Anaheim, CA 92806

714-567-6206

7. Cleveland National Forest

This southernmost of California's national forests rambles over more than 420,000 acres, blanketing an arc of mountains that marches 135 miles, from the Los Angeles basin to within five miles of the Mexican border. Consisting of three separate units, whose western boundaries lie 10 to 30 miles from the Pacific coastline, the forest is a mix of scrubby chaparral, oak and coniferous woodlands, broad meadows, lush canyons, natural hot springs, boulder-strewn creeks with idyllic swimming holes, waterfalls, and craggy peaks more than 6,000 feet high. Mountain lions, bighorn sheep, wild pigs, bobcats, and diamondback rattlesnakes make their homes in the wild corners of the forest, bald and golden eagles swoop from the skies in search of prey, and an astonishing number of rabbits and quail thrive in the dense undergrowth of the chaparral.

Trabuco Ranger District, the only unit of Cleveland National Forest that lies completely within the 100-mile radius established for this book, extends south from Corona to the northern boundary of Camp Pendleton Marine Base (described elsewhere). Although some 12 million people live within a 2- to 3-hour drive of this part of the forest, relatively few visitors come here because access can be difficult. Only one primary road, the east-west Ortega Highway, crosses Trabuco. Other roads penetrate the forest's boundary from all sides, but many are in poor condition and best traveled on foot or in four-wheel-drive vehicles.

Nearly 50,000 acres in the southern reaches of this district, including the remote canyon carved out by San Mateo Creek, have been proposed for wilderness designation. Caspars Wilderness Park and Starr Ranch Audubon Sanctuary (both described elsewhere) adjoin Trabuco District along its western border and are accessible from the Ortega Highway. Just off the Ortega Highway as it emerges from the forest's eastern edge is Lake Elsinore State Recreation Area, which offers swimming, boating, fishing, and camping.

About 20 miles to the southeast lies the Palomar District of Cleveland National Forest, site of the world-famous Palomar Observatory. The Hale Telescope, housed in a giant silvery dome twelve stories high, boasts a collecting mirror 200 inches in diameter and was until recently the largest optical telescope on earth. The Soviets now have a telescope with a 236-inch mirror, but it has been plagued by defects. By contrast, the 530-ton Hale Telescope is so well engineered that it can be repositioned with a $\frac{1}{12}$ horse power electric motor and can study celestial objects up to 15 billion light years, or about 90 trillion miles, distant. (To give this some perspective, an astronaut traveling the speed of light—186,000 miles per second—could cover the same distance in a little over 15 billion years.) The five-domed observatory, owned by the California Institute of Technology, is a research facility, and visitors are not permitted to look through any of several telescopes on the grounds. Visitors may, however, view the Hale Telescope from a glassed-in balcony (kept at nighttime temperatures to avoid distortion of the mirror's face) and tour Greenway Museum, where displays include stunning photographs of observatory sightings. Perched near the top of 6,140-foot-high Palomar Mountain, the observatory is reached via the Highway to the Stars, a winding road that provides far-reaching views of the earth as well as of the sky. Motorists pass through a cool forest of black oak and Coulter pine, whose cannonball-size cones are the heaviest in the world— woods so lushly beautiful that they once inspired a visiting professor to describe Palomar as a "hanging garden" with "forests a king would covet."

Because of the mountain's popularity, several recreation areas have been established nearby—three campgrounds and a picnic area operated by the U.S. Forest Service, Palomar Mountain State Park (described elsewhere), and 2-acre Palomar County Park, a San Diego County property with picnic tables and a small campground.

Tucked away in the northwest corner of the Palomar Ranger District is a 15,934-acre sprawl of pristine land known as the Agua Tibia Wilderness, where deep canyons slice through rugged mountainous terrain. Much of the chaparral that covers approximately 69 percent of this area has for more than 100 years miraculously escaped the wildfires so prevalent in Southern California, and the vegetation is unusually mature and dense. Some manzanitas, common chaparral plants classified botanically as shrubs, here form trunks and attain treelike heights of 20 feet; other species of shrubs are 14 to 16 feet tall. The upper slopes of the mountains are shaded by oak and pine forests.

The interesting but little-known Indian Flats, located in a remote portion of the Palomar District east of Palomar Mountain, is a combination of mountains and desert.

Approximately two thirds of the Palomar Ranger District, including Palomar Mountain and the Agua Tibia Wilderness, lies within a 100-mile radius of Los Angeles. Further to the south, the remainder of Palomar and the entire Descanso Ranger District, the forest's third area, offer such attractions as the Pine Creek Roadless Area, proposed for wilderness designation; one of the oldest ranger stations in California (built in 1911 of hand-hewn logs); three mountaintop fire lookout stations that are at times open to the public; the Pine Hills area, which flourished as a gold-mining center in the late nineteenth century; a demonstration area where public agencies and private landowners are testing various methods of chaparral management (chaparral covers nearly one half of the Golden State), and some unusual trees, including the world's largest Witches Broom (a pine tree deformed by a parasite), the Cuyamaca and Tecate cypress, and the Jeffrey pine, whose largest cones grow nearly a foot long.

Twice annually, the forest is bright with color. The vast expanses of chaparral, a study in gray most of the year, can be glorious when spring blossoms transform them; and in autumn, the oak woodlands flaunt the flamboyant hues of the season.

Winter visitors can often frolic in snow at elevations above 3,000 feet, and in summer elevations above 5,000 feet provide a cool retreat from the heat of the lowlands.

Hiking and Horseback Riding

The Pacific Crest National Scenic Trail (described elsewhere) passes through the Palomar and Descanso districts. Other forest trails range in length from about 1¼ to 8 miles one-way, although several have spurs that provide longer hikes, and some enter rugged terrain. One of the best-maintained trails in the Trabuco

District is the Chiquito Basin Trail, which partially parallels a shady creek and passes a small but lovely waterfall. Part of the challenge of the San Mateo Canyon Trail is getting to the trailhead, but those who do can trek through the heart of the proposed wilderness area—a stunningly beautiful place dotted with 200-year-old oaks and lush masses of ferns. In the Palomar District, the north-south Pine Flat Trail that traverses the Agua Tibia Wilderness offers panoramic views of the ocean to the west and the Santa Rosa Mountains to the east. Another trail begins at Observatory Campground and climbs through a conifer forest to Palomar Observatory. All three districts feature self-guided nature trails, and a special orienteering course has been constructed near Blue Jay Campground in the Trabuco District (instruction packet available from the district office). All trails except nature trails are also open for horseback riding; horses may be rented at various locales around the forest's perimeter. Both hikers and equestrians are required to obtain permits, issued free of charge, before entering wilderness areas. During the summer season, naturalists offer such special activities as night hikes, horseback interpretive tours, star parties, and auto tours.

Fishing

Fishing within forest boundaries is limited; there are no lakes, and most streams are seasonal. Several creeks in the Trabuco District are stocked with rainbow trout each spring, and the San Luis Rey River in the Palomar District offers spring and winter trout fishing. The Lake Elsinore State Recreation Area just east of the Trabuco District and Lakes Henshaw and Sutherland along the eastern border of the Palomar District provide additional opportunities for anglers.

Camping

Several campgrounds with tables, toilets, grills, and drinking water are available in each of the forest's three districts; most are suitable for both tents and trailers. No hookups, dump stations, or showers. Tenaja Campground in the Trabuco District provides hitching posts for equestrians. The Yerba Santa Campground in the Descanso District, usually open mid-May to October, is reserved for handicapped people and families and friends who accompany them. Remote country camping is allowed in designated areas if you first obtain a free permit. Campground seasons and fees vary; remote sites are free. State, county, and private recreation areas within or just outside forest boundaries provide additional campsites, some with full hookups.

Picnicking

Developed picnic areas are located in scenic settings along major forest roads. All feature tables and toilets; drinking water and grills are available at some.

How to Get There: Cleveland National Forest's three districts occupy parts of Orange, Riverside, and San Diego counties. To reach Trabuco District from LA, go south on I-5 to San Juan Capistrano and turn east onto CA 74 (Ortega Hwy.); follow CA 74 through Caspars Wilderness Park into the forest. To reach Palomar District from LA, go south on I-5 to CA 91 (Riverside Fwy.). Go east on CA 91 to I-15, then take I-15 south to CA 76. Follow CA 76 east to Rincon Springs, where CA 76 is joined by San Diego County Hwy. S6 coming up from the south. Continue on 76/S6 for about 5 miles, when the two roads again separate. Follow S6 (the Highway to the Stars) north to its terminus at Palomar Observatory in the forest's Palomar District. To continue south to Descanso District, return via S6 to CA 76, and turn east, following CA 76 to its junction with CA 79. Turn south, and continue on CA 79 to I-8 (along the way, signs indicate spur roads that lead into the forest). CA 79 and I-8 meet within the Descanso District. To learn more about recreation opportunities in and near the forest, visitors can obtain free literature and, for a nominal fee, a forest map at any of the information sources given at the end of this listing. Ranger stations located throughout the forest can also supply information; look for signs.

Forest lands accessible at all times. Free. Some parts of the Trabuco and Palomar districts are closed to public access during fire season (from July 1 to the first good rain, usually during the fall but sometimes as late as December). Headquarters and district offices open 8–4:30 Monday through Friday; closed some holidays. The Hale Telescope visitors' gallery at Palomar Observatory is open 9–4 daily; museum open

9–4:45 daily; closed Christmas Eve and Christmas Day. Both free.

For Additional Information:
Information Officer
Cleveland National Forest Headquarters
880 Front St., Room 6-S-5
San Diego, CA 92188

619-293-5050

Trabuco District Office
Cleveland National Forest
Room 926, New Federal Bldg.
34 Civic Center Plaza
Santa Ana, CA 92701

714-836-2144

Palomar District Office
Cleveland National Forest
332 S. Juniper St.
Escondido, CA 92025

619-745-2421

Descanso District Office
Cleveland National Forest
P.O. Box 309
(2707 Alpine Blvd.)
Alpine, CA 92001

619-445-6235

Palomar Observatory
c/o Astronomy Department
California Institute of Technology
1201 E. California Blvd.
Pasadena, CA 91125

619-742-3476 (Observatory)
818-356-6811 (Institute)

8. Idyllwild Park

Nestled in the midst of the spectacular San Jacinto Mountains, this 202-acre county park is primarily a celebration of nature. Visitors have been coming here since 1921 to enjoy the fresh, clean air, sweet with the scents of white fir, black oak, Ponderosa pine, and incense cedar, and to unwind in the cool mountain atmosphere.

Surrounded on all sides by the San Bernardino National Forest (described elsewhere), the park is alive with wildlife. Bighorn sheep, bobcats, and mountain lions roam remote mountain areas, while squirrels, raccoons, coyotes, and skunks venture a bit closer to developed parts of the park. Five species of birds—the white-headed woodpecker, the mountain quail, the spotted owl, Williamson's sapsucker, and Lawrence's goldfinch—are found in larger numbers in the San Jacinto Mountains than anywhere else on the North American continent.

From May through September, park naturalists lead campfire programs. More naturalist programs, as well as nature trails and special displays, are offered at the Idyllwild Visitor Center.

Hiking

Miles of hiking trails are in and around the park. The popular Deer Springs Trail, which begins across the highway from the Idyllwild Visitor Center parking area, leads into the Mount San Jacinto State Park and Wilderness (described elsewhere). During its 3½-mile length, it climbs 2,000 feet in elevation, passes through a pine-fir forest, and provides splendid views.

Gray fox

Camping

Idyllwild Park has thirty-six sites for tent campers, thirty-seven sites for RVs up to 20 feet long, and nineteen sites for RVs up to 30 feet long. Tables and fireplaces at each site; modern restrooms close at hand. Camping fee is lower Tuesday–Thursday. Reservations accepted; phone 714-787-2553 on weekdays.

How to Get There: Located in west central Riverside County. From LA, take CA 60 east to I-10. Continue east on I-10 to Banning. At the 8th St. exit in Banning, go south on 8th St. to Lincoln Ave. and turn east. Proceed a few blocks on Lincoln Ave. to CA 243 (S. San Gorgonio St.) and turn south. Follow CA 234 south for about 25 miles to the Idyllwild Visitor Center on the right side of the highway, approximately 1 mile northwest of the village of Idyllwild. To reach Idyllwild Park, continue past the Visitor Center into the village of Idyllwild and turn west on County Park Rd. Follow County Park Rd. for approximately 1 mile into the park.

Visitor Center open 9–6 Wednesday–Sunday during the summer, 10–4 Monday–Friday, and 10–5 Saturday and Sunday rest of year. Free. Park open daily, year-round, sunrise to sunset. Nominal vehicle admission fee.

For Additional Information:
Idyllwild Visitor Center
P.O. Box 341
Idyllwild, CA 92349

714-659-3850 (Visitor Center)

Riverside County Parks Department
P.O. Box 3507
Rubidoux, CA 92519
714-787-2551

9. Indian Canyons of Palm Springs

The 32,000-acre Agua Caliente Indian Reservation in and around Palm Springs is laced with trails that lead through the desert landscape to some spectacular canyons. Palm, Andreas, and Murray canyons, which lie on Indian land just south of Palm Springs, are among the most popular natural attractions in the area. Lush, cool, and serene, they are true desert oases.

More than 3,000 native Washingtonia (desert fan) palms, some over 90 feet tall and estimated to be 300 to 400 years old, line a spring-fed stream in Palm Canyon. Except for isolated trees in Arizona and southernmost California, this species of palm is found growing wild only in the remote gorges and ravines within the drainage regions of the Salton Sea, a large, saltwater lake that lies approximately 40 miles southeast of Palm Springs.

Washingtonia palms also grow, although fewer in number, in Andreas and Murray canyons. In addition to the palms, the stream that flows through Andreas Canyon is edged by dense growths of sycamores, alders, willows, and tangles of wild grapevines. You'll also see towering cliffs, dramatic rock formations, and several small caves that invite exploration. Cottonwood, sycamore, and wild tamarack trees are interspersed among the streamside palms in wild and primitive Murray Canyon, where a band of wild horses makes its home. Each autumn, the canyons' deciduous trees offer a rare sight in the desert—a splash of brilliant fall color.

The verdant beauty of a fourth canyon—Tahquitz —and its 60-foot waterfall was captured on film in the original *Lost Horizon*.

Late winter and early spring, when the wildflowers are popping, and again in November, when temperatures are mild, are good times to visit.

Hiking and Horseback Riding

Hikers and riders both may follow the trails through Palm, Andreas, and Murray canyons. The 15-mile-long trail in Palm Canyon, bordered for two miles by towering palm trees, is one of the most scenic in the region; it's rated moderately difficult. The 1-mile-long Andreas Canyon trail, a favorite with equestrians, and the 3-mile-long Murray Canyon trail are easy walks; a pool of water in Murray Canyon looks inviting on a warm day, but swimming is not advisable because of sharp, protruding rocks. Take some drinking water along, and be on the lookout for scorpions and rattlesnakes.

All trail distances listed are one-way; although the

trails are on Indian land, they are maintained by Desert Riders, a local equestrian group, in cooperation with the city of Palm Springs. Horses may be rented locally.

Picnicking

Picnic areas, maintained by the Agua Caliente Indians, are available in Palm, Andreas, and Murray canyons.

How to Get There: Located in central Riverside County, south of Palm Springs. From LA, go east on I-10 to CA 111 and turn southeast to Palm Springs. CA 111 is known as Palm Canyon Dr. in Palm Springs. Near the south end of Palm Springs, CA 111 makes a sharp turn to the east and becomes E. Palm Canyon Dr. Do not make this turn, but instead continue straight ahead on S. Palm Canyon Dr., which leads to the Indiana reservation and its canyons. Look for signs along the way. You may drive to the mouths of Palm and Andreas canyons, but you'll have to walk about ½ mile to the mouth of Murray Canyon. Horses may be rented locally.

Since the trail to Tahquitz Canyon is not well maintained, check locally for trail conditions and directions before starting out. Hikers and riders begin this trek at different access points.

Reservation gates open 9–4 daily, early September through mid-June. Nominal entrance fee to reservation. Seasonal hiking and equestrian passes are available.

For Additional Information:
Convention & Visitors Bureau
Airport Park Plaza
255 N. El Cielo Rd., Suite 315
Palm Springs, CA 92262

619-327-8411

Desert Riders
113 Camarillo St.
Palm Springs, CA 92262

(No phone)

Indian Canyons Information
Agua Caliente
960 E. Tahquitz Way
Palm Springs, CA 92262

619-325-5673

10. Joshua Tree National Monument

Although Joshua trees are found throughout the Mojave Desert uplands, they grow most profusely within the boundaries of Joshua Tree National Monument. An extraordinary stand of these fascinating plants sprawls across the western reaches of this half-million-acre parkland, set aside by a 1963 presidential proclamation to ensure the preservation of a forest with no trees (the Joshua is actually a giant lily).

Like most inhabitants of the desert, Joshua trees grow slowly—a maximum of 3 inches a year during the first ten years of life and 1½ inches per year thereafter. Only a rare few grow taller than 40 feet. The gangly plants and their oddly angled branches, which leaf out only at the tips, create spectacular silhouettes against the stark desert landscape. Although individual plants do not flower every year, the Joshua forest is alive with blooms in the spring (except during unusually dry years), when clusters of creamy-white blossoms 8 to 14 inches long appear among the leaves.

The Mojave Desert, which here ranges in elevation from 3,000 to 5,000 feet above sea level and receives an average of 6 to 10 inches of precipitation annually, provides an ideal habitat for the Joshua tree. In the drier climate and lower elevations of the Colorado Desert, which occupies the eastern half of the monument, the creosote bush is the dominant vegetation. The contrasting environments of the high and low deserts, along with five oases that rise like verdant islands from a desolate sand sea, attract a remarkable assortment of wildlife. Coyotes, burrowing owls, bighorn sheep, bobcats, golden eagles, roadrunners, tarantulas, scorpions, and sidewinder rattlesnakes are just a few of the species that thrive here. The amazing kangaroo rat, often seen around campgrounds at night, can survive a normal lifetime without a single drink of water, obtaining all the moisture it needs from seeds in its diet.

Bizarre rock formations and soaring heaps of gigantic boulders, tossed with abandon by ancient earth forces, provide rock scrambling at its best. Rockhounds can trace the entire spectrum of geologic history on stone faces that date from the Precambrian era to the present.

Unusual plants grow everywhere here, but rarely in great concentration. One exception is the thick stand of Bigelow cholla that grows in a cactus garden near the transition zone formed by the meeting of the Mojave and Colorado deserts. The plant's nickname, "teddy bear," belies the fact that the cholla is the spiniest of all cacti. Be sure to heed the "Don't Touch" signs. At the slightest pressure, one of the cholla's barbed balls may break off and adhere to your skin.

Some 450,000 acres in Joshua Tree National Monument are designated wilderness, but a network of roads—some paved, some dirt—leads visitors to a variety of park features. At an overlook atop the Little San Bernardino Mountains is a superb, sweeping view of the Colorado Desert, low-lying Salton Sea, lush date gardens of the Coachella Valley, and 11,499-foot-high San Gorgonio Mountain, the tallest peak in southern California. On a clear day, you can see all the way to Mexico.

The desert is most popular in the spring when, if winter rainfall has been sufficient, multitudes of showy wildflowers flood the somber landscape with brilliant blooms. But if you like your desert lonesome, come another time. Fall and winter days are bright and pleasant, and even summers are usually comfortable, especially in the high desert.

Whatever the time of year, your visit will be more enjoyable if you first stop at the main Visitor Center. In addition to the free park brochure, there are displays and an array of literature that provides information applicable not only to Joshua Tree National Monument, but to the entire southwestern desert as well. Ranger-conducted activities are available on spring and fall weekends.

Hiking and Horseback Riding

A 35-mile-long trail for hikers and equestrians extends east from Black Rock Canyon campground to a point just south of the Oasis Visitor Center. Other hiking trails are 1½ to about 9 miles in length. One of the most popular is a 4-mile trail that leads from Cottonwood Springs Campground to Lost Palms Oasis, which harbors more than 100 fan palm trees. Other trails lead to carefully preserved historic sites, including two gold mines and a ranch, and some pictographs. Shorter walks are provided by several nature trails. Hiking through isolated backcountry is fantastic experience, but before setting out, stop at a Visitor Center to learn wilderness rules and purchase a topographic map.

Camping

Eight campgrounds contain more than 525 family campsites for tents and trailers; no showers. A fee is charged at two modern campgrounds that offer tables, fireplaces, flush toilets, and nearby drinking water; one has a disposal station. Primitive sites with tables and pit toilets are free; drinking water must be carried in. Horses are permitted at Black Rock Canyon and Ryan campgrounds. Seasons vary, but some campgrounds are open all year. There is also unlimited backcountry camping; regulations available at Visitor Centers.

Joshua tree at Joshua Tree National Monument

Picnicking

Day-use picnic areas are scattered throughout the park; drinking water must be carried in to most of them.

How to Get There: Joshua Tree National Monument straddles the San Bernardino/Riverside county line just south of Twenty-nine Palms; only the western portion of the monument lies within the 100-mile radius covered by this book. From LA, go east on I-10, through Banning, to CA 62. Head north and then east on CA 62 to Utah Trail, which lies just east on Twenty-nine Palms. Take Utah Trail south a short distance to park headquarters and the Oasis Visitor Center. Look for signs along the way.

Park open at all times; headquarters and Oasis Visitor Center open 8–5 daily, year-round. Hours vary for other Visitor Centers in park. Free.

For Additional Information:
Joshua Tree National Monument
74485 National Monument Dr.
Twenty-nine Palms, CA 92277

619-367-7511

11. La Jolla Sea Caves

For centuries, the sea has pounded relentlessly against the sandstone cliffs of La Jolla Cove, patiently reshaping the precipitous rock walls and carving out a series of caves. Most of them are accessible only from the sea, but one may be entered through the La Jolla Cave and Shell Shop.

Passing through a tunnel hand-hewn from the rock, you descend 133 steps to a large grotto. Lights play against walls streaked with colorful mineral deposits and imbedded with fossils that date back more than 200,000 years. Sometimes fish, temporarily trapped by the whims of the tides, scurry about in pools of water that cover part of the cave's floor. The waters of La Jolla Cove, visible through the mouth of the cave, are part of the San Diego–La Jolla Ecological Reserve.

Although there is no beach at the foot of these cliffs, you can enjoy a panorama of ocean and caves from the Coast Walk, a path that winds along the blufftops for about ½ mile.

How to Get There: Located just north of downtown San Diego. From LA, go south on I-5 to the La Jolla Village Dr. exit. Follow La Jolla Village Dr. east to Torrey Pines Rd. and turn south. Proceed on Torrey Pines Rd. to Prospect St., turn east onto Prospect St., and go to Coast Blvd., a loop road on the seaward side of Prospect St. The Cave and Shell Shop is located at 1325 Coast Blvd. The Coast Walk may be entered from Torrey Pines Rd. (just east of its intersection with Prospect St.) or in the Goldfish Point area adjacent to the shell shop. You'll also find some steps at Goldfish Point that lead down to tidepools. Parking on area streets.

Shell shop and the cave entrance open 10–6 Monday–Saturday, 11–6 Sunday, mid-June to mid-September; 10–5 Monday–Saturday, 11–6 Sunday the rest of the year; closed Thanksgiving, December 25. Nominal admission fee to cave. Everything else is free.

For Additional Information:
La Jolla Cave and Shell Shop
1325 Coast Blvd.
La Jolla, CA 92037
619-454-6080

12. Moorten's Botanical Garden

If you want to tour the deserts of the world in a single afternoon, Moorten's Botanical Garden is the place to go. This 2½-acre garden contains desert plants from the southwestern United States, Mexico, Central and South America, Africa, and the Gobi Desert in Asia— more than 2,000 varieties in all.

Each plant is labeled and grows alongside other plants from its native habitat. In the Baja California section, visitors stroll past elephant and ironwood trees. Joshua trees grow in the Mojave Desert area, while the Chihuahuan Desert of Texas is represented by an ocotillo forest. Plants in the South American corner of the garden include some from the Galapagos

Islands. Several types of desert wildlife inhabit the grounds, and peacocks roam about displaying their lustrous plumage.

Among the special highlights here are the world's first cactarium, a prehistoric garden complete with dinosaur footprints and petrified logs, and a prickly pear fruit orchard. Geology buffs will be particularly intrigued by exhibitions of some extraordinary geodes and such semiprecious stones as amethyst, turquoise, topaz, and garnet.

Pat Moorten and her late husband, "Cactus Slim," who together founded the garden in 1938, became so renowned as desert authorities that Walt Disney asked them to design the desert wonderland area of Disneyland. The Moortens also landscaped Disney's former Palm Springs home, as well as the homes of Frank Sinatra, Frank Lloyd Wright, Lily Pons, Bing Crosby, and President Dwight D. Eisenhower. Mrs. Moorten resides within the garden and is often on hand to personally greet visitors.

Specimens of many plants, bejeweled rocks, and fresh fruits born by some of the cacti may be purchased on the grounds. The public is also welcome to use a botanical library and research center by advance reservation.

How to Get There: Located in Riverside County near the south edge of Palm Springs. From LA, go east on I-10 to CA 111 and turn southeast. CA 111 leads into Palm Springs, where it becomes Palm Canyon Dr. Continue through town to a point where CA 111 makes a sharp turn to the east. Do not turn, but proceed straight ahead on S. Palm Canyon Dr. for a short distance. The garden is located on the west (right) side of the road.

Open 9–5 daily. Nominal admission fee; under 7 free.

For Additional Information:
Moorten's Botanical Garden
P.O. Box 851
(1701 S. Palm Canyon Dr.)
Palm Springs, CA 92264

619-327-6555

13. Mount San Jacinto State Park and Wilderness

Just west of Palm Springs and the sun-baked Coachella Valley, the San Jacinto Mountains jut thousands of feet into the air. The mountain air is pine-scented and pure, and temperatures in the summer are about 40 degrees cooler than on the desert floor from which the mountains rise so abruptly. From December through April, snow at the highest elevations may be as deep as 10 feet, and below-zero temperatures are common. The northeast face of the San Jacinto Range plunges 9,000 feet in less than 6 miles, making it one of the sheerest escarpments in North America.

In the heart of this spectacular region, the state of California has established a 13,521-acre park, most of which is managed as wilderness. Elevations here range from 5,500 feet above sea level near park headquarters to 10,804 feet atop the craggy peak of Mount San Jacinto, the second highest point in southern California. Some 250 species of plants thrive here, including dense growths of such evergreens as incense cedars, white firs, and lodgepole pines. Mountain lions, bobcats, coyotes, deer, skunks, gray foxes, mountain quails, and bighorn sheep inhabit the park's

Tahquitz Rock, Mount San Jacinto State Park and Wilderness

high country, and bald eagles are sometimes spotted soaring overhead.

Since the park is otherwise accessible only on foot or horseback, many visitors choose to come here via the Palm Springs Aerial Tramway, which carries passengers 2½ miles from Valley Station (elevation 2,643 feet) in Chino Canyon to Mountain Station (elevation 8,516 feet) in the northeast section of the park. At the top is a chalet with a restaurant and several observation terraces, where you can share a view that John Muir once called "the most sublime spectacle to be found anywhere on this earth." Two cars, which hold eighty passengers each, operate continually throughout the day.

The state park is bounded on three sides by the San Bernardino National Forest (described elsewhere), which provides additional recreational opportunities.

Hiking and Horseback Riding

Approximately 54 miles of trails traverse the park, some joining trails in the San Bernardino National Forest. Trails are accessible from both the western edge of the park and, for those on foot, from the top of the aerial tramway. Also at the top of the tramway are two short loop trails, one ⅔ of a mile long and another 1½ miles long. A portion of the Pacific Crest National Scenic Trail (described elsewhere) runs north and south through the western portion of the park. Before entering the wilderness, hikers and equestrians must obtain a free permit. Permits for day use are available on the day of entry at park headquarters or at Long Valley Ranger Station near the top of the tramway; permits for overnight use must be obtained at least ten days in advance by writing to, or in person at, park headquarters. Horses may be rented in the village of Idyllwild near the park's western border; all feed for horses must be packed in. If you enter the wilderness in winter, be sure you're properly equipped.

Camping

Two developed campgrounds are located adjacent to CA 243 near Idyllwild. Idyllwild Campground is situated in a pine forest adjacent to park headquarters.

It offers thirty-three sites with tables, stoves, food cabinets, and nearby bathrooms with hot showers; no hookups. Stone Creek Campground, 6 miles north of Idyllwild, has fifty sites with tables, stoves, pit toilets, and drinking water. Maximum vehicle length at each is 24 feet. Fees charged at both campgrounds. Reservations required for summer weekends and accepted for any summer stay; contact Ticketron outlets throughout the state. Campgrounds are open year-round, although all facilities are not available in the winter at Idyllwild and the road at Stone Creek is not plowed when snow is on the ground. Six primitive, hike-in campgrounds in the wilderness are free, but permits are required.

Winter Sports

Cross-country skiers and snowshoers take to the trails in winter; rental equipment and instructions are available at the tramway station.

How to Get There: Located in Riverside County. To reach park headquarters, go east from LA on CA 60 to I-10. Continue east on I-10 to Banning. At the 8th St. exit in Banning, go south on 8th St. to Lincoln Ave. and turn east. Proceed a few blocks on Lincoln Ave. to CA 243 (S. San Gorgonio St.) and turn south. Follow CA 234 south for about 26 miles to park headquarters on the west side of the highway just north of Idyllwild. Headquarters open 8 A.M.–5 P.M. every day of the year; park open at all times. Free.

To reach the aerial tramway, continue east from Banning on I-10 to CA 111. Follow CA 111 southeast to Tramway Rd. at the Palm Springs city limits and turn west. Tramway Rd. ends at the tramway's Valley Station. Look for signs. Tram rides begin at 10 A.M. Monday–Friday and at 8 A.M. Saturday and Sunday; last trip departs Valley Station at 7:30 P.M., returns at 9:15 P.M. Closed month of September (after Labor Day) for maintenance. Fee.

For Additional Information:
Mount San Jacinto State Park
P.O. Box 308
Idyllwild, CA 92349
714-659-2607

Palm Springs Aerial Tramway
P.O. Drawer FF
Palm Springs, CA 92263
619-325-1391

14. O'Neill Regional Park

O'Neill Regional Park nestles in beautiful Live Oak and Trabuco canyons in the Santa Ana Mountains. With an elevation of only 1,000 feet above sea level, the park offers mild winters and warm, dry summers. Its 669 acres of grassy meadows, shrub-covered hillsides, oak and sycamore woodlands, and canyon floor watered by two seasonal streams make it one of the most topographically varied parks in Orange County.

The northwest corner of the U-shaped park, wild and undeveloped, is designated a natural area. Coyotes, badgers, ground squirrels, rattlesnakes, bobcats, and fox live here. Golden eagles are sometimes spotted overhead, and on occasion a cougar wanders by.

Land is currently being acquired for another Orange County park that will adjoin O'Neill Park on the south and be managed as a wilderness area. To be called Arroyo Trabuco, the new park contains the largest and richest stand of California sycamores in the world. Some of the giant trees are 21 feet in diameter. O'Neill Park rangers can provide up-to-date information.

Hiking and Horseback Riding

Two extensive nature trails and a scenic equestrian trail meander through the park. Self-guiding trail brochures, available at the park office, acquaint hikers with significant natural and geographical features of the area. Trails are also planned for Arroyo Trabuco Park.

Camping

Some 250 tent and RV sites are provided in two areas —one along Trabuco Creek, the other at a higher elevation; picnic tables, drinking water, restrooms with showers, generous shade cover. One dump station is available. Facilities for riders and their mounts are provided in an equestrian camping area near the riding trail.

Picnicking

A day-use picnic area accommodates both families and groups; picnic tables, barbecue grills, drinking water, restrooms, and a large turf area. Nearby are a softball diamond, horseshoe pits, and playground equipment. A concession building near the park entrance sells quick foods.

How to Get There: Located in eastern Orange County. From LA, go south on I-5 to El Toro Rd. (Co. Hwy. 18) and turn northeast. Proceed on El Toro Rd. for about 7½ miles to Live Oak Canyon Rd. (Co. Hwy. 19). Turn east and continue about 3 miles to the park entrance on the south (right) side of Live Oak Canyon Rd.

Open daily 7 A.M.–10 P.M. April–September, 7 A.M.–sunset October–March. Nominal vehicle admission fee.

For Additional Information:
O'Neill Regional Park
30892 Trabuco Canyon Rd.
Trabuco Canyon, CA 92678

714-858-9365

Environmental Management Agency of
Orange County
Recreation Facilities Operations
10852 Douglass Rd.
Anaheim, CA 92806

714-567-6206

15. Orange County Marine Institute

Young Richard Henry Dana came here in 1834 as a crew member of the *Pilgrim*, a sailing ship that transported raw hides from California to New England to supply the leather goods industry. Deeply impressed by the picturesque cove and steep, sandstone bluffs, he later described it in *Two Years Before the Mast* as "The only romantic spot on the coast." Today, Dana

Point bears his name, and a replica of the *Pilgrim* is anchored in the harbor.

The 120-foot, two-masted brig is the major attraction of the Orange County Marine Institute, an oceanographic studies center situated along the shoreline in the west basin of Dana Point Harbor. Primarily an educational facility, the institute offers a wide variety of public and school programs, including some aboard the *Pilgrim*. Within the institute's modern headquarters building, the Ocean Gallery displays marine art, nautical treasures, aquariums filled with living specimens, and the skeleton of a gray whale.

Each February, a Festival of Whales celebrates the annual migration of the gray whales, whose southward route lies 5 minutes offshore. Whales can be seen along this part of the coast from January through most of March, and during that time, whale-watch cruises depart Dana Point Harbor several times daily. In addition to spending an hour or two among the whales, passengers are often treated to close-up views of sea lions sunning themselves on the rocks just outside the harbor. The Marine Institute also sponsors whale-watching expeditions of several days' duration to the lagoons of Baja.

Just north of the institute, at the foot of the bluffs, are some marvelous tide pools to explore at low tide. They're protected as part of the Dana Point Harbor Marine Life Refuge (see Orange County's Marine Life Refuges, described elsewhere).

How to Get There: Located in southern Orange County. From LA, go south on I-5 to the Crown Valley Pkwy. Take the parkway southwest to CA 1 (Pacific Coast Hwy.) and turn southeast to 24200 Dana Point Harbor Rd. Proceed through Dana Point to Del Obispo Rd. on the eastern edge of town and turn toward the sea. Del Obispo Rd. curves around Dana Point Harbor and ends near the Marine Institute. Parking on site.

Open 10–3:30 Monday–Saturday, year-round (hours may vary); closed major holidays. Free admission to exhibits and tide pools; fee for some programs.

For Additional Information:
Orange County Marine Institute
P.O. Box 68
Dana Point, CA 92629

714-496-2274

16. Orange County's Marine Life Refuges

Until a few years ago, visitors to Orange County's tide pools carried away bucketloads of marine life to stock home aquariums. Not only did most of the specimens thus collected fail to survive elsewhere, but the tide pools were being rapidly depleted of life. To preserve these fragile ecosystems, where life flourishes as in no other part of the land or sea, the County Board of Supervisors established a string of marine life refuges along the Orange County coast.

The result is a series of natural aquariums where today's visitors can view a rich and colorful array of aquatic plants and animals. Anemones, algae, starfish, mussels, sea urchins, hermit crabs, sea hares, and rockweed are just a few of the species that thrive in this habitat.

Scientists estimate that, even with total protection, the tide pools will take as long as twenty-five years to return to their original levels of production, so it is extremely important that nothing be disturbed or removed within refuge boundaries. Also, for your own safety, be aware of changing water levels and wear thick clothing with safe shoes, such as tennis shoes or boots, for protection against sharp rocks.

How to Get There: Located in the rocky areas of Orange County's coastline between Newport Beach on the north and Dana Point on the south. Names of the refuges, from north to south, are Newport Beach, Irvine Coast, Laguna Beach, South Laguna, Niguel, Dana Point, and Doheny Beach. From LA, go south on I-5 to CA 55 (Costa Mesa-Newport Fwy.) and turn southwest. Proceed on CA 55 to CA 1 (Pacific Coast Hwy.) and turn southeast. All refuges are accessible from CA 1; for exact directions, contact one of the agencies whose names follow this listing.

Open at all times. Free.

For Additional Information:
Environmental Management Agency of
Orange County
Recreation Facilities Operations
10852 Douglass Rd.
Anaheim, CA 92806

714-567-6206

State of California
Department of Fish & Game, Region 5
300 Golden Shore
Long Beach, CA 90802

213-590-5132
213-590-5111

Doheny State Beach
34320 Del Obispo Rd.
Dana Point, CA 92629

714-496-6171

17. Palm Springs Desert Museum

Located near the heart of Palm Springs, the Desert
Museum is devoted to the natural and human history
of the Coachella Valley, as well as the visual and performing arts.

Activate an extensive desert diorama by pressing a
button, and see such creatures as the roadrunner, bobcat, and coyote in both daytime and nocturnal environments. Push other buttons to see Salton Sea bird
life, desert wildflowers, Indian artifacts, and a desert
slide show. Two sunken gardens provide lovely back-
drops for some of the museum's sculptures.

Nature field trips, varying in subject and length, are
conducted on a regular basis; check for schedule.

Slightly beyond the radius covered by this book,
but well worth seeing, is the Living Desert Reserve—
a branch of the Palm Springs Desert Museum near
Palm Desert. This 1,200-acre interpretive center contains nature trails, acres of botanical gardens that
re-create different North American deserts, a walk-
through aviary, a care center for injured or orphaned
wildlife, outdoor animal exhibits of desert wildlife
(including bighorn sheep, coyotes, and raptors) in en-
closures, a bookstore, and a Visitor Center.

Hiking and Horseback Riding

A 1-mile-long nature trail begins at the museum's
north parking lot and ascends 1,000 feet in elevation
along its westward route up a mountainside. It termi-
nates at the Lykken Skyline Trail, a 2-mile-long path
that rises vertically 900 feet from its southern to its
northern terminus. These trails are physically de-

manding for hikers; wear comfortable shoes, carry water at all times, and avoid hiking during July and August heat. Markers along the museum trail and part of the Lykken Trail are keyed to a trail guide available at the museum. Only hikers may use the museum trail; Lykken Trail, maintained by an organization called Desert Riders, is open to both hikers and equestrians. Vehicle parking is available at the Desert Museum; horse-trailer parking available on Ramon Rd. at the southern terminus of the Lykken Trail. Horses may be rented locally.

The Living Desert Reserve offers several miles of self-guiding hiking and nature trails; some pass by a bighorn sheep study area, where sheep are sometimes spotted among the rocks.

Picnicking

Enjoy a picnic with a scenic view. Tables at the junction of the museum and Lykken trails overlook Palm Springs and the Coachella Valley. A picnic area is also available in a palo verde grove at the Living Desert Reserve.

How to Get There: From LA, go east on I-10 to CA 111 and head southeast to Palm Springs. CA 111 is also known as Palm Canyon Dr. in Palm Springs. Continue on CA 111 to Tahquitz-McCallum Wy. and turn west. Proceed to Museum Dr. and turn north (right) to the museum on the west (left) side of the road.

To reach the Living Desert Reserve, continue through Palm Springs on CA 111 to Portola Ave. in Palm Desert. Turn south and follow Portola Ave. to the reserve on the east (left) side of the road.

Museum open 10–4 Tuesday–Friday and 10–5 Saturday–Sunday, late September to mid-June; closed rest of year, as well as January 1, Easter, Thanksgiving, December 25. Reserve open 9–5 daily, September 1 to mid-June. Admission fee to both; under 8 free at museum, under 17 free at reserve (if accompanied by an adult).

For Additional Information:
Palm Springs Desert Museum
101 Museum Dr.
Palm Springs, CA 92262
619-325-7186

Living Desert Reserve
47-900 S. Portola Ave.
Palm Desert, CA 92260

619-346-5694

Desert Riders
113 Camarillo St.
Palm Springs, CA 92262

(No phone)

18. Palomar Mountain State Park

Once thousands of band-tailed pigeons nested on the slopes of the mountain on which this 1,900-acre park is located, and so the Spaniards named it Palomar, or "place of the pigeons." Most of the pigeons are gone now, but a wide variety of other birds and small animals live here, and mountain lions are occasionally spotted in the more remote areas.

Lush forests such as these—dense stands of tall pines, firs, and cedars, nurtured by an annual rainfall of about 40 inches—are more often found in the Sierra Nevada Mountains that slice through the northern part of the state than in southern California. The mountain air is crisp and cool, and on clear days you can stand at observation points more than 5,000 feet above sea level and look out over ocean and desert.

The world-famous Palomar Observatory, located on the highest point of 6,100-foot Palomar Mountain, is just east of the park in the Cleveland National Forest (described elsewhere). National forest lands surround Palomar State Park and provide many additional recreational opportunities.

Hiking and Horseback Riding

Short, easy trails wind throughout the park, including some that are suitable for horseback riding. The longest trail extends about 2 miles one-way, the shortest about ½ mile.

Camping

Thirty family campsites accommodate recreational vehicles up to 21 feet long. Each site has a table, stove, and food locker; restrooms, hot showers, and laundry tubs are nearby.

Picnicking

Located in a grove of magnificent incense cedars near one of the park's observation points, the Silver Crest Picnic Area features thirty-six tables and wood stoves. No gathering of wood; wood must be brought in or purchased at park. Drinking water and restrooms close at hand. More picnic tables and stoves are near the shores of Doane Pond.

Fishing

Doane Pond is stocked with trout; fishing is especially good during the winter, spring, and early summer.

How to Get There: Located in northwestern San Diego County. From LA, take I-5 south to CA 76 in Oceanside. Go east on CA 76, through Pala and beyond the town of Pauma Valley, for about 7 miles, to Co. Rd. S6. If you are driving an automobile, turn northeast (left) and follow S6 to Co. Rd. S7, then turn northwest (left) and proceed into the park on S7. If you are in a camper or pulling a trailer, you'll find the going much easier if you stay on CA 76, past S6, to the junction of CA 76 and S7 near Lake Henshaw. Turn northwest (left) onto S7 and proceed into the park.

Open daily, year-round, during daylight hours. Nominal vehicle admission fee.

For Additional Information:
Palomar Mountain State Park
Palomar Mountain, CA 92060

714-742-3462

California Department of Parks & Recreation
Montane Area Headquarters
c/o Cuyamaca Rancho State Park
12551 State Hwy. 79
Descanso, CA 92016

619-765-0755

19. Point Fermin Park

Point Fermin Park, perched atop a rocky bluff on the Palos Verdes Peninsula, commands one of the finest views in southern California—a 180-degree panorama of the Pacific Ocean and Los Angeles Harbor. During winter months, visitors come to watch migrating gray whales through coin-operated telescopes. A whale-watching station in the park provides information and a free twenty-minute movie on the gentle cetaceans.

The beautifully landscaped, 37-acre park is also the home of the only wooden lighthouse still standing along the California coast. Built in 1874, it remained in operation until 1942. The Victorian-style structure now serves as the residence of the park superintendent and is closed to the public, but its picturesque setting amid dense foliage and emerald lawns near the cliff's edge makes it a favorite with photographers.

Two trails lead from the bluff to the rocky shoreline, where you'll find some excellent tide pools to explore.

Picnicking

Picnic tables with barbecue pits sit among the trees. The view is splendid, and water, restrooms, and playground are close at hand.

How to Get There: From LA, take I-110 (Harbor Fwy.) south until it ends at Gaffey St. in San Pedro. Continue south on Gaffey St. until it ends at Paseo Del Mar. Point Fermin Park is on the south side of this intersection. To reach the beach trails, turn west onto Paseo Del Mar. The first trail is accessible from the juncture of Paseo Del Mar and Roxbury St. Continue west to the second trail, accessible from the juncture of Paseo Del Mar and Leland St.

Park open at all times; whale watch station open 9–4 Saturday–Sunday. Free.

For Additional Information:
Superintendent
Point Fermin Park
807 Paseo Del Mar
San Pedro, CA 90731

213-548-7756

City of Los Angeles
Department of Recreation & Parks
200 N. Main St., 13th Floor
Los Angeles, CA 90012

213-485-5515

20. Prado Basin Park

Located along the north bank of the Santa Ana River, Prado Basin Park covers nearly 2,000 acres, 143 of which are developed. Its chaparral-covered hills overlook one of the few natural riparian areas remaining in southern California.

Because water flows in the Santa Ana all year long (unusual in this region) and because the entire park is managed as a biological preserve, many species of wildlife make their home here. Ducks winter on the river, and birds of prey seek cover in the chaparral. Many small birds, including the lazuli bunting and blue grosbeak, nest among the willows that line the riverbank.

You can learn about the park's history—both natural and human—at the Visitor Center. Among the displays are artifacts of the Gabrielino Indian culture and samples of the gold, silver, tin, and coal that once were mined in this area.

Hiking

More than 4 miles of interpretive trails lead throughout the park. A trail guide is available for the Willow Flat Nature Trail, which begins at the Visitor center and meanders through the riparian area.

Picnicking

Two picnic areas have tables, grills, drinking water, and restrooms. One also offers a playground and small wading lake.

How to Get There: Located in northwestern Riverside County. From LA, take I-5 south to CA 91. Follow CA 91 east to Corona. At the Main St./Hamner Ave. exit, go north for about ½ mile to River Rd. and turn northwest. River Rd. crosses the Santa Ana River within the park. At McCarty Rd. near the park's northern boundary, turn west (left) and proceed a short distance to the park entrance on the south (left) side of McCarty Rd.

Park open 8 A.M.–sunset daily. Nominal vehicle admission fee. Visitor Center open 9–5 Wednesday–Sunday (hours may vary). Free.

For Additional Information:
Prado Basin Park
(14600 River Rd.)
Corona, CA 91720

714-735-7130

County of Riverside Parks Department
P.O. Box 3507
Riverside, CA 92519

714-787-2551

21. Quail Botanic Gardens

Although they cover just 30 acres, these gardens in Encinitas contain a wide variety of plants. One trail offers a glimpse at the native landscape of pre-twentieth-century California, while another leads through a subtropical fruit area that features such hard-to-find species as kiwis, macadamia nuts, and cherimoyas. Still others pass collections of cacti, bromeliads, begonias, ferns, azaleas, fuschias, iris, aloes, bamboo, palms, pines, and flowering eucalyptus trees. Along the way, you'll also see many rare and unusual plants, including the Hong Kong orchid tree, the Del Mar manzanita, the boojum tree, the Torrey pine, and the dragon tree.

The California quail, for which the gardens are named, Brewer's blackbird, red-tailed hawk, and Anna's hummingbird are on hand to delight bird watchers.

Trail guides are available at the registration desk near the parking lot.

Picnicking

A few picnic tables are available, but no fires are permitted.

How to Get There: Located in west central San Diego County. From LA, take I-5 south to the Encinitas Blvd. exit in Encinitas and turn east. Take Encinitas Blvd. to Quail Gardens Dr. and turn north. The garden is on the west side of the street at 230 Quail Gardens Dr. Parking on site.

Open 8–6 daily, April–October; 8–5 the rest of the year. Free admission; nominal vehicle parking fee.

For Additional Information:
Quail Gardens Foundation
230 Quail Gardens Dr.
Encinitas, CA 92024

619-436-3036

Quail Botanic Gardens

22. Ralph B. Clark Regional Park

From 1956 to 1973, the California Division of Highways used approximately 350 million cubic yards of
sand and gravel from this site in the construction of
two freeways. The rich fossil beds exposed in the excavation process proved so significant that Orange
County acquired 85 acres of land here to preserve the
discovery. Now a regional park, this site was the location of a great marsh some 10,000 years ago. At least
seventy different forms of life, including the mammoth, ground sloth, and ring-tailed cat, lived in this
area. The only known specimens of the prehistoric
slender-limbed camel ever discovered in western
North America, as well as the largest collection of
fossilized pond turtles in southern California, were
unearthed here.

A free-standing wall displays simulated fossil imprints of some of the prehistoric animals that once
roamed the Los Coyotes foothills. Many of the fossils
found here are displayed in the park's museum.

Opened to the public in 1981, the park is still under
development, with such features as an ongoing dig
planned for the future.

Picnicking

Several large picnic areas are scattered throughout the
park, some near the shore of a 3-acre lake; restrooms,
drinking water, play fields, and playground equipment are nearby.

How to Get There: Located in northern Orange
County. From LA, go south on I-5 to CA 39 (Beach
Blvd.). Take CA 39 northeast to Rosecrans Ave. and
turn east for approximately ¼ mile. The park is located on both sides of Rosecrans Ave. in the 8800
block, but most of the developed area, including the
administration building, is on the south side of the
road.

Open daily 7 A.M.–10 P.M. April–September, 7
A.M.–sunset the rest of the year. Nominal vehicle admission fee.

For Additional Information:
Ralph B. Clark Regional Park
8800 Rosecrans Ave.
Buena Park, CA 92621

714-670-8045

Environmental Management Agency of
Orange County
Recreation Facilities Operations
10852 Douglass Rd.
Anaheim, CA 92806

714-567-6206

23. San Diego Wild Animal Park

You can take a wildlife tour of Africa and Asia in a single afternoon at the San Diego Wild Animal Park. The 1,800-acre sanctuary is home to some 3,600 animals, many of them representing species nearly extinct in the wild. A branch of the San Diego Zoo (described elsewhere under Balboa Park), the Wild Animal Park is particularly noted for its contributions to cheetah research and its attempts to establish a breeding group of California condors (a native species, but one of the rarest birds in the world and critically endangered).

Animals roam freely in settings similar to their native habitats. Visitors may explore the preserve via a monorail safari or, from May through October, join a photo caravan in an open-air truck, both accompanied by knowledgeable guides. For the more ambitious, there's a 1¾-mile-long hiking trail specially designed to provide close-up views of lions, tigers, cheetahs, giraffes, and rhinos.

An African village near the park entrance houses a variety of animal exhibits, special attractions such as animal shows, shops, and restaurants. Children especially enjoy the petting zoo, animal care center, and elephant rides. Occasionally, you can watch elephants getting a bath.

The park's botanical collection, valued at nearly $1 million, is almost as varied and exotic as the animal population. Tours may be arranged for some of the gardens.

How to Get There: Located in San Diego County, approximately 30 miles north of San Diego. From LA, take I-5 south to Oceanside. Then go east on CA 78 to Escondido, south on I-15 to Via Rancho Pkwy., and east to the park. Follow signs.

Open 9–9 mid-June through Labor Day, 9–5 March through mid-June and post–Labor Day through October, 9–4 rest of year. Entrance fee includes monorail, all shows, and exhibits; ages 2 and under free. Extra charge for photo caravans; advance reservations a must.

For Additional Information:
San Diego Wild Animal Park
15500 San Pasqual Valley Rd.
Escondido, CA 92027

619-234-6541
619-480-0100

24. Santa Catalina Island

Santa Catalina has been a favorite playground for southern Californians for years, a mountainous silhouette on the Los Angeles horizon that promises all the romance and allure of an island getaway just 25 miles from the mainland. Beyond Avalon, the small, charming resort town near the ferry terminal, are more than 40,000 acres of wildly beautiful terrain.

Rugged mountain peaks that climb as high as 2,100 feet form the backbone of the 21-mile-long island. Cutting through them are deep canyons that lead to sheltered coves and sun-drenched beaches at the edge of the sea.

Buffalo, wild boar, deer, and wild goats roam the lofty interior. At the El Rancho Escondido, nestled in a lush valley, you may watch purebred Arabian horses raised and trained there go through their paces.

Migrating California gray whales pass close to Santa Catalina in late winter and early spring, and seals play on offshore rocks most of the year. Just off the island's lee shore are the magnificent Undersea Gardens, an exotic underwater world filled with bright fish and luxuriant vegetation. Catalina's flying fish, up to 18 inches long, frequent the eastern coastline from May into September.

Located 1.7 miles from downtown Avalon, the 40-acre Wrigley Botanic Garden features cacti, succulents, and a collection of endemic Catalina flora. It offers a succinct preview of the more than 390 native plant species (including an unusual ironwood and seven others found nowhere else in the world) that grow wild elsewhere on the island.

During summer months, the Catalina Island Marine Institute sets up an interpretive center in the heart of Avalon where you may view and touch a variety of marine life in shallow aquariums. The Institute, located at Toyon Bay on the island's east shore, offers a variety of summer sea camp programs for ages eight and up. Among the skills participants can learn while exploring Catalina's marine and island environments are scuba diving, snorkeling, underwater photography, sailing, and seamanship.

You may explore the island on foot, atop a bicycle or horse, in an electric minicar, or on one of several bus and tram tours. Boat cruises permit visitors to see many parts of the shoreline that are otherwise inaccessible.

If you want to spend a weekend or vacation here, there are hotels, apartments, and housekeeping cottages in Avalon and campsites elsewhere on the is-

Santa Catalina Island

land (advance reservations required for all overnight accommodations).

Some 86 percent of Santa Catalina is owned by a nonprofit foundation known as the Santa Catalina Island Conservancy. The Los Angeles County Parks & Recreation Department maintains an office on the island and helps The Conservancy manage its acreage for conservation and recreational purposes.

Hiking, Bicycling, and Horseback Riding

Many miles of undeveloped trails, ranging from jeep trails to fire roads and rough paths, crisscross and loop throughout the island. Some provide easy walking; others lead up steep slopes and are recommended for experienced hikers only. Although drinking water is available in places, hikers are advised to carry some water with them on hikes of more than one hour; backpackers will find campsites at designated areas along the way. Almost any smooth road or path on the island is open to bicyclists, who may make advance arrangements with cross-channel carriers to bring their own bikes along or rent them at one of several places in Avalon. Permits, issued free of charge by several agencies on the island, are required for hiking and bicycling in Santa Catalina's interior. Picturesque bridle trails lace through the mountains and valleys; rental horses are available at a stable in Avalon.

Boating and Fishing

Rowboats, outboards, and inboards are available for rent. Several fully crewed boats may be chartered by small groups; many offer sailing instructions. Regularly scheduled boat cruises carry sightseers along Catalina's jagged coastline; one of the most popular is the glass-bottom boat tour of the Undersea Gardens. If you travel to Catalina in your own boat, you'll find first-come, first-serve moorings at Avalon and Two Harbors, a small settlement approximately 15 miles north of Avalon.

Fishermen can choose from a variety of bait and tackle, then rent or charter a boat to angle for the bonito, marlin, white or black sea bass, broadbill, swordfish, tuna, mackerel, yellowtail, barracuda, and albacore that inhabit offshore waters. Pier fishing is also popular.

Swimming and Diving

A small beach in the heart of Avalon offers free swimming from Easter week through October, but is usually very crowded on weekends. Lockers, beach chairs, back rests, umbrellas, and paddle boards are available for rent. The island's network of roads and trails leads to numerous other beaches along the shoreline; still more beaches are accessible only by boat. Catalina's clear waters and abundant sea life make this an ideal area for skin and scuba divers; diving equipment, including air, can be rented or purchased year-round in Avalon.

Camping

Camping is restricted to five designated campgrounds. All offer tent sites, drinking water, toilet facilities, and grills; some have showers and fire rings. Nominal fees are charged, and sites must be reserved in advance. Reservations for the three southernmost campgrounds can be made through the Los Angeles County Parks & Recreation Department in Avalon or for the two northernmost campgrounds through the Catalina Cove & Camp Agency.

Picnicking

Free public picnic grounds with tables, barbecue braziers, and volleyball courts are located on Cabrillo Crescent in Avalon (ask for permission to use them at the Harbor Master's Office on Pleasure Pier). Private picnic grounds with rustic shelters, tables, and outdoor barbecue ovens are situated on Avalon Canyon Rd. beyond the stables (obtain a permit and pay fee at the Visitor's Information & Services Center in downtown Avalon). Food and groceries may be purchased in Avalon.

How to Get There: Most visitors cross the 20-some miles of water between Catalina and the mainland by boat. Three companies currently operate passenger boats between the mainland and Santa Catalina Island. Catalina Channel Express (Box 1391, San Pedro, CA 90733; phone 213-519-1212) provides daily service year-round from Catalina Terminal in San Pedro to Avalon and Two Harbors. Catalina Cruises (Box 1948, San Pedro, CA 90733; phone 213-775-6111, 213-832-4521, or 714-527-7111) sails from Catalina

Terminal in San Pedro and from Long Beach Terminal; daily, year-round service to Avalon; daily during summer, weekends rest of year to Two Harbors. Catalina Passenger Service (400 Main St., Balboa, CA 92661; phone 714-673-5245) departs from Balboa Pavilion near Newport Beach; daily service April through October to Avalon, available for group charters rest of year.

All three mainland embarkation points can be reached by heading south from downtown LA on I-405 (San Diego Fwy.). To reach Catalina Air-Sea Terminal in San Pedro, proceed to junction of I-405 and Harbor Fwy. (CA 11). Turn south on Harbor Fwy. to the Harbor Blvd. turnoff; take this turnoff and continue for about 1 mile, following signs to terminal located under the Vincent Thomas Bridge. To reach Long Beach Terminal, go to junction of I-405 and Long Beach Fwy. (CA 7); head south on Long Beach Fwy. to Downtown Long Beach exit; take this exit a short distance, bearing right, to Golden Shore exit; take Golden Shore Blvd. and follow signs to terminal. To reach Balboa Pavilion, go to junction of I-405 and Beach Blvd. (CA 39) near Huntington Beach; take Beach Blvd. south to the Pacific Coast Hwy. (CA 1); turn southeast and proceed to Balboa Blvd.; turn right to Balboa Pavilion; look for signs along the way.

Several air charter services provide transportation from mainland airports (especially Long Beach Airport) to Catalina's Airport-in-the-Sky. Helitrans offers regularly scheduled helicopter service from Catalina Terminal in San Pedro; for reservations, phone 213-548-1314 or 1-800-262-1472 from other California area codes.

One-way crossings by boat take less than 2 hours; by air, about 20 minutes. Reservations are advisable for all trips.

Since there is so much to see and do on Catalina Island, it's best to plan your trip well in advance.

For Additional Information:
Santa Catalina Island Conservancy
P.O. Box 2739
Avalon, CA 90704

213-510-1421

Catalina Island Chamber of Commerce
P.O. Box 217
Avalon, CA 90704

213-510-2266

Santa Catalina Island
Visitor's Information & Services Center
P.O. Box 737
Avalon, CA 90704

213-510-2500

Los Angeles County Department of Parks &
  Recreation
P.O. Box 1133 (Island Plaza)
Avalon, CA 90704

213-510-0688

Catalina Cove & Camp Agency
P.O. Box 5044
Avalon, CA 90704

213-510-0303

Catalina Island Marine Institute
P.O. Box 796
Avalon, CA 90704

213-510-1622

25. Santiago Oaks Regional Park

Nestled among the gently rolling foothills of the Santa
Ana Mountains, this 125-acre wilderness park is
home to mountain lions, mule deer, coyotes, and bobcats. It is also one of the prime bird-watching areas in
Orange County—a mecca for more than 130 species,
including the California quail, great blue heron, red-
tailed hawk, and an occasional great horned owl. California sycamores, coast live oak, walnut, and arroyo
willow trees shade the land, and Santiago Creek
meanders through the heart of the park.

Once part of a ranch, Santiago Oaks still bears some
imprints of past owners. The rock dam across Santiago Creek was built in 1892. An extensive grove of
ornamental trees thrives on the north side of the
creek, and a 9-acre Valencia orange grove near the
park entrance still produces fruit. Next to the orange

grove is an old ranch house that has been converted to a nature center.

In keeping with the park's wilderness designation, facilities are limited, and visitors may enter only on foot or horseback.

Hiking and Horseback Riding

Several miles of hiking and horse trails lead through the wildest parts of the park and join the county's extensive Anaheim Hills Trail System. A loop nature trail begins near the nature center. Park rangers offer nature walks of varying lengths on a regular basis.

Picnicking

One small picnic area with nearby restrooms, drinking water, and a swing set for the youngsters is located next to the nature center; no grills.

How to Get There: Located in northeastern Orange County. From LA, take I-5 south to CA 22 (Garden Grove Fwy.). Go east on CA 22 to CA 55 (Costa Mesa/ Newport Fwy.). Follow CA 55 north to Chapman Ave. and turn east. Take Chapman Ave. to Santiago Canyon Rd. (S18). Go north and west on Santiago Canyon Rd. until you reach Windes Dr. on the north side of the highway. Turn north onto Windes Dr. and continue to Oak Ln. (Windes Dr. jogs to the east here.) Turn east onto Oak Ln., then almost immediately turn north again onto Windes Dr. Continue on Windes Dr. until it ends near the park entrance. Look for signs along the way. Limited parking in posted lots near the park gate and along the creek side of Windes Dr. Enter the park only on foot or horseback; the nature center and picnic area are a short distance from the gate.

Park open 7 A.M.–sunset daily; nature center open 9–4 daily (closed some major holidays). Both free.

For Additional Information:
Santiago Oaks Regional Park
2145 N. Windes Dr.
Orange, CA 92669

714-538-4400

Environmental Management Agency of Orange
County
Recreation Facilities Operations
10852 Douglass Rd.
Anaheim, CA 92806

714-567-6206

26. Scripps Aquarium-Museum

Scripps Institution of Oceanography, a branch of the
University of California, is world renowned for its
oceanographic research around the globe. In La Jolla,
within sight of the Pacific, the Scripps Aquarium-
Museum offers the public an insight into the institution's work. Exhibits on tidal fluctuations, beach ecology, ocean archaeology, the geology of sea basins, and
marine life are among the fascinating displays.

More than 150 species of fish and 80 invertebrates
are kept in some twenty tanks. Major feeding times
are on Wednesday and Sunday at 1:30 P.M.

Video cameras provide underwater views of two
marine preserves—the San Diego–La Jolla Underwater park and Ecological Reserve and the Scripps
Shoreline–Underwater Reserve—established along
the nearby coast to protect sea and shore life.

Also in the museum is an excellent scientific book-
shop.

Outside, a man-made tide pool that generates its
own waves captivates visitors of all ages.

How to Get There: Located on the grounds of the
Scripps Institution of Oceanography in La Jolla. From
LA, go south on I-5. Exit west onto La Jolla Village
Dr., go to N. Torrey Pines Rd., and turn north to La
Jolla Shores Dr. Turn west and proceed to the aquar-
ium on the ocean side of the road.

Open 9–5 daily. Free.

For Additional Information:
Scripps Aquarium A-007
Scripps Institution of Oceanography
University of California, San Diego
8602 La Jolla Shores Dr.
La Jolla, CA 92093

619-534-4086

27. Seal Beach National Wildlife Refuge

Established in 1972 to preserve one of the largest remaining coastal wetland systems in southern California, Seal Beach National Wildlife Refuge lies within the boundaries of the U.S. Naval Weapons Station near Long Beach. The tidal creeks, salt marshes, mud flats, and sloughs that make up the 977-acre sanctuary provide habitat for more than 100 species of birds, including the endangered California least tern, brown pelican, and what is believed to be the largest population of light-footed clapper rails in the state. During fall and winter months, thousands of migratory birds visit the area.

No visitors are allowed on the refuge itself, but the wetlands can be viewed from Sunset Aquatic Park, an Orange County property that adjoins the refuge's southern boundary.

Boating and Fishing

A small boat harbor, open to the public, is available at the Sunset Aquatic Park marina. There are no rentals, but an eight-lane concrete launch ramp is available 24 hours a day for a fee. No boats allowed on refuge waters.

Such species as bonito, halibut, jacksmelt, mackerel, perch, and rock bass enter harbor waters by way of Anaheim Bay. Best fishing months are generally April through September.

Picnicking

Picnic tables dot emerald lawns and overlook the harbor at Sunset Aquatic Park.

How to Get There: Located in the community of Seal Beach in Orange County, just southeast of Long Beach. From LA, go south on Harbor Fwy. (I-110/CA 11) to CA 1. Turn east and proceed on CA 1 to Seal Beach Blvd., which runs off to your left. Stay on CA 1, but just after passing Seal Beach Blvd., you'll see the marshes of Seal Beach National Wildlife Refuge, also on your left. Continue on CA 1 to Warner Ave. and turn east. Proceed on Warner Ave. to Bolsa Chica St. and turn north. Follow Bolsa Chica St. to Edinger Ave. and turn west. Edinger Ave. ends in

Sunset Aquatic Park. The wildlife refuge can be seen on the north side of Edinger Ave. both before and after you enter the park.

   Sunset Park is open 24 hours a day, year-round. Free.

For Additional Information:
Seal Beach National Wildlife Refuge
c/o Kern National Wildlife Refuge
P.O. Box 219
Delano, CA 93216

805-725-2767

Sunset Aquatic Park
P.O. Box 538
Sunset Beach, CA 90742

213-592-2833 (Marina)

28. Sea World

An intimate look at the creatures that inhabit the world's seas is offered at Sea World, a 110-acre aquarium that features an array of marine life, animal shows, rides, and an imaginative playground with nautical themes for children under fourteen.

   Penguin Encounter, a unique exhibit that is also the largest penguin breeding and research facility in the world, houses seven species of the flightless birds in refrigerated comfort. Visitors glide by on a moving sidewalk while viewing the penguins both above and under water through a wall of glass. You may also look a full-grown shark in the eye, pet a whiskery walrus, feed a dolphin, and hold a delicate starfish in your hand.

   Presiding over it all is Sea World's superstar—Shamu, the killer whale, who cavorts through the water carrying a trainer on his back and sometimes favors visitors with a wet kiss.

How to Get There: Located on the south shore of Mission Bay, just northwest of downtown San Diego. From LA, drive south on I-5 and exit west onto Sea World Dr. Follow signs.

   Open 9–dusk daily. Entrance fee; under 3 free. Ticket offices close 1½ hours earlier than park.

For Additional Information:
Sea World
1720 South Shores Rd.
San Diego, CA 92109

619-226-3901

29. Sherman Library and Gardens

The botanical collections of the 2-acre Sherman Gardens feature tropicals, subtropicals, cacti, and succulents displayed in a serene setting of fountains and sculptures. Among the highlights are a shade garden, a rose garden, a desert garden, a tropical conservatory, a fish pond stocked with brightly colored koi, an outdoor tea garden where refreshments are served, and a garden shop. Plantings in major flower beds and hanging baskets are changed several times a year to reflect seasonal colors.

The Sherman Library, a specialized research center, is devoted to the history of the American Southwest, particularly during the last 100 years.

How to Get There: Located in coastal Orange County, just south of Newport Beach. From LA, take I-5 south to I-605. Continue south on I-605 to I-405, then south on I-405. Exit at MacArthur Blvd., head southwest to CA 1 (Pacific Coast Hwy.), and turn southeast (left) for about two blocks to 2647 East Coast Hwy. The gardens are on the ocean side. Parking on site.

Gardens open 10:30–4 daily. Tea Garden open 10:30–3 Saturday–Monday. Library open 9–5 Monday–Friday. All closed Thanksgiving, December 25, January 1. Nominal admission fee; under 12 free.

For Additional Information:
Sherman Library and Gardens
2647 East Coast Hwy.
Corona del Mar, CA 92625

714-673-2261

30. South Coast Botanic Garden

Once people came here to dump trash. Now they come to marvel at the beauty of the South Coast Botanic Garden, one of the first botanical gardens in the world to be developed above a sanitary landfill.

In 1959, when Los Angeles County officials authorized an experiment in land reclamation on this site, three and one-half million tons of refuse were buried under 3 feet of topsoil. Today, the land is lush with vegetation—more than 200,000 plants representing some 2,000 different species from every continent except Antarctica—and horticulturists and government administrators from all over the world come to study the feasibility of starting a similar project in their own lands.

Interlacing trails and paths lead throughout the garden's 87 acres and to a man-made lake. On a clear day, the terrain's high points provide a panoramic view of Los Angeles.

Birds, too, are attracted to the garden, and more than 200 species have been sighted here. Guided Audubon nature walks, open to anyone, are conducted monthly.

The buildings that make up the Visitors Center near the entrance are set on 40-foot pilings to allow for any movement experienced as the earth settles over the old dump.

Picnicking

Several picnic tables are scattered over the lawn at the south end of the parking lot.

How to Get There: Located on the Palos Verdes Peninsula, southwest of downtown LA. From LA, take I-110/CA 11 (Harbor Fwy.) south to CA 1 (Pacific Coast Hwy.). Go west on CA 1 about three miles to Crenshaw Blvd. and turn south. The garden's entrance is on the east side of Crenshaw.

Open 9–5 daily; closed December 25. Nominal entrance fee; under 5 free. Tram tours available for extra charge on Saturday and Sunday.

For Additional Information:
South Coast Botanic Garden
26300 Crenshaw Blvd.
Palos Verdes Peninsula, CA 90274

213-377-0468

31. Starr Ranch Audubon Sanctuary

Starr Ranch, owned and managed by the National Audubon Society, is a mix of flower-strewn grasslands,
dense oak woodlands, streams shaded by giant sycamores, arid ridges, and rugged canyons. Mountain
lions find sanctuary on these 3,900 acres, as do bobcats, coyotes, mule deer, and gopher snakes. Among
the more than 120 species of birds that nest and feed
here are seventeen types of raptors, including golden
eagles and the endangered black-shouldered kite.
This remarkable variety makes Starr Ranch one of the
richest bird of prey habitats in the entire country.
Hummingbirds and woodpeckers may be seen at any
time.

Although Starr Ranch is managed as a nature preserve and is stringently protected, visitors will find
opportunities for outdoor recreation in the adjacent
Cleveland National Forest and Caspars Wilderness
Park (both described elsewhere).

How to Get There: Located in the western foothills
of the Santa Ana Mountains in eastern Orange
County; bordered by Cleveland National Forest along
part of its northern and eastern boundaries and by
Caspars Wilderness Park (an Orange County park)
along its southern boundary. Entrance is through Caspars Wilderness Park; you will receive exact directions when you make your arrangements to visit here.

Open at all times, but visitation is limited and advance arrangements must be made through the resident manager. Guided group tours are scheduled each
spring and summer; reservations required. No set fee,
but contributions are greatly appreciated.

For Additional Information:
Resident Manager
Starr Ranch Audubon Sanctuary
P.O. Box 967
Trabuco Canyon, CA 92678
714-858-0309

32. Stewart Mine

This nation's finest pink tourmaline mine, world-
famous among gem and mineral collectors, is bored

into a hillside in northwestern San Diego County. When the mine was first seriously worked in the early part of this century, the entire output was exported to the empress of China. Today the mine produces gemstones for sale all over the world.

Although Stewart Mine is most noted for its brilliant pink specimens, it also yields green, black, and variegated pink-and-green tourmalines, the last of which is extremely rare.

No tours are currently being given, but check at the time of your visit.

How to Get There: Stewart Mine is located northeast of the town of Pala. From downtown LA, go south on I-5 to CA 91, then east on CA 91 to I-15, south on I-15 to CA 76, east on CA 76 to Pala, and north on Co. Hwy. S16 for approximately 1 mile. The road to Stewart Mine runs east off S16.

For Additional Information:
Gems of Pala
Box 382
Pala, CA 92059

619-742-1356

33. Torrey Pines State Reserve and Beach

At Torrey Pines State Reserve, you can see a stand of the rarest pine tree in the nation. The Torrey pine grows naturally in only two places in the world—on Santa Rosa Island in Channel Islands National Park (described elsewhere) and in and around this 1,000-acre reserve. Perched on the sides of deep ravines and atop 300-foot bluffs that edge the sea, bent and twisted by the elements into grotesque shapes, the picturesque pines frame striking panoramas of the Pacific coastline. These unique trees vary in height from 10 to 100 feet (the growth of those nearest the sea is stunted by the wind and salt air), and a tree's root system may be more than three times as long as a tree is tall. Despite encroaching development and harsh weather conditions, nearly 10,000 trees flourish in this rugged reserve's two noncontiguous units, with the finest groves found in a natural area known as the Torrey Pines Natural Preserve.

A second natural area in the park, the Los Penasquitos Marsh Natural Preserve, encompasses a portion of one of the few remaining salt marsh and lagoon areas in southern California. Such rare and endangered species as the light-footed clapper rail and the California least tern make their home here, and many more birds pause to rest during migratory periods. All together, about 200 avian species have been sighted in the marsh and the park's uplands. They share the land with a proliferation of rabbits and rodents, as well as a few gray foxes, coyotes, mule deer, and rattlesnakes.

Botanical species are even more varied. Some 300 types of native plants, including several found nowhere else, grow within reserve boundaries.

Geology buffs will want to examine the stone bluffs, composed of ancient marine beach terraces that are imbedded with fossil invertebrates. The colorful sandstone strata of Broken Hill are 20 to 30 million years old.

Just south of the reserve, when weather conditions are right, hang gliders launch their crafts from the cliff's edge and brighten the sky with their brilliant hues.

Special times to visit include January, when migrating gray whales (see Whale Migration, described at the end of the book) are often spotted just offshore. The red blooms of the Torrey pines are an interesting mid-February happening, closely followed by a spectacular progression of wildflowers from early March to late April. Large coveys of California quail are often seen just after the park opens on fall and winter mornings. And if you wish to sense the suspended-in-time feeling that this seaside wilderness evokes, come in the early morning, when swirling mists still cling to the land and the air is filled with the fresh scent of a new day.

Flora and fauna lists are available at the reserve office/museum, and special interpretive exhibits are located at several points in the park.

Only about 400 people are allowed on the reserve at any one time. On weekends, when the park usually fills to capacity, visitors should plan to arrive no later than midmorning.

Hiking

A number of trails ranging in length from ½ mile to 1½ miles lead throughout the park, including the noncontiguous area to the north of the main reserve. The popular Guy Fleming Trail, featuring many uniquely shaped pines and panoramas of the Pacific, is an easy 0.7-mile loop within the Torrey Pines Natural Preserve; with luck, you may spot a bottlenose dolphin or, in the winter, migrating gray whales. High Point Trail, the park's shortest at 0.4 mile, passes some of the reserve's oldest living trees and leads to an ocean view. Beginning at the parking lot, the 1.1-mile Beach Trail offers visitors the opportunity to study the park's geological features and intertidal life. Trails in the Extension Area wind among Torrey pines and provide views of the Los Penasquitos Lagoon, the ocean, and, on occasion, some rare plant and animal life. These and other trails are easily located on the park folder. You can also wander along the beach, 4½ miles long within the park, but be sure to check the tide tables before starting out on a long walk. Some stretches of beach are completely underwater at high tide. Park naturalists guide nature walks at 1:30 P.M. each Saturday and Sunday.

Picnicking

A picnic area is located near the park entrance. No open fires permitted, but concrete fire rings are provided, and visitors may bring along portable stoves. Restrooms are close at hand. Picnicking is also allowed all along the beach, but you must carry out your litter.

Water Sports

Swimming, surfing, and skin diving are popular, but stay alert. Riptides sometimes occur along this part of the coast.

Perch, corbina, and croaker lure surf fishermen to the area.

How to Get There: Located in western San Diego County, about 1 mile south of Del Mar. From LA, go south on I-5 to Del Mar Heights Rd. and turn west. Proceed on Del Mar Heights Rd. to Camino Del Mar Rd. (CA 21) and turn south. Continue about 4 miles to the park's main entrance on the west side of the road (along the way, Camino Del Mar Rd. changes its name to Torrey Pines Rd.).

Open daily; reserve 9 A.M.–sunset, museum 11 A.M.–4 P.M., beach 8 A.M.–sunset. Vehicle admission fee daily during summer and on weekends year-round.

For Additional Information:
Torrey Pines State Reserve & Beach
c/o San Diego Coast Area Office
Department of Parks & Recreation
State of California
P.O. Box 38
(2680 Carlsbad Blvd.)
Carlsbad, CA 92008

619-755-2063 (State Reserve)

34. Whale Migration

It is a celebration of life, an extravaganza of nature that is unequaled in the world. Each winter, approximately 12,000 gray whales leave their summer feeding grounds in Arctic waters off Alaska and migrate some 6,000 miles to breed and calve in the warm, shallow lagoons of Baja California. From November through February, they travel southward in small groups, following a route that lies about ½ mile offshore.

Thousands of whale-watchers, armed with binoculars, telescopes, and high-powered cameras, crowd high coastal bluffs hoping for just a glimpse of the telltale water spout of a great whale. Thousands more opt for whale-watching boat excursions, generally from two hours to eight days in duration. Still others don scuba gear and dive into the water to swim among the gentle giants (a full-grown whale may be up to 45 feet long and may weigh as much as 50 tons).

Southern California's premier onshore whale-watching spot is Cabrillo National Monument (described elsewhere) near San Diego, but many points of land that jut into the sea, as well as Anacapa and Santa Barbara islands (both described elsewhere under Channel Islands National Park), also offer good views.

The whales can usually be seen in peak concentrations during January. When the last of the southbound stragglers near Baja in late February or early March, they meet the first of the northbound migrants. Most whales choose a route farther from the coast for their journey back to northern waters and thus can't be seen from shore. Excursion boats head out to this more distant route from late February through mid-April to give whale-watchers the opportunity to observe mother whales with newborn calves.

In addition to expeditions run by commercial operators, boat trips are sponsored by private organizations, universities, museums, and nature societies. Nearly all require reservations well in advance. A list of all such trips is too lengthy to include here, but the following places can provide you with up-to-date information on expeditions based in their respective areas.

For Additional Information:
American Cetacean Society
National Headquarters
P.O. Box 2639
San Pedro, CA 90731

213-548-6279

American Cetacean Society
Celia Taylor
5125 Cape May Ave.
San Diego, CA 92107

619-226-6007

San Diego Natural History Museum
P.O. Box 1390
San Diego, CA 92112

619-232-3821, Ext. 22

Orange County Marine Institute
P.O. Box 68
Dana Point, CA 92629

714-496-2274

Cabrillo Marine Museum
3720 Stephen White Dr.
San Pedro, CA 90731

213-548-7562

Long Beach Area
Convention and Visitors Council
180 E. Ocean Blvd., Suite 150
Long Beach, CA 90802

213-436-3645

Greater Los Angeles Visitors & Convention Bureau
515 S. Figueroa St.
Los Angeles, CA 90071

213-689-8822

Newport Beach Convention & Visitors Bureau
P.O. Box 2417
Newport Beach, CA 92663

714-675-7040

Chamber of Commerce
P.O. Box 1578
(512 4th St.)
Oceanside, CA 92054

619-722-1534

Convention & Visitors Bureau
400 Esplanade Dr.
Oxnard, CA 93030

805-485-8833

Chamber of Commerce
1215 N. Catalina Ave.
Redondo Beach, CA 92077

213-376-6911

San Diego Convention & Visitors Bureau
1200 Third Ave., Suite 824
San Diego, CA 92101

619-232-3101

Chamber of Commerce
P.O. Box 167
(390 W. 7th St.)
San Pedro, CA 90733

213-832-7272

Conference & Visitors Bureau
22 E. Anapamu
Santa Barbara, CA 93101

805-966-9222

Santa Monica Convention and Visitors Bureau
P.O. Box 5278
Santa Monica, CA 90405

213-393-7593

Ventura Visitor & Convention Bureau Information
Center
785 S. Seaward Ave., Suite B
Ventura, CA 93001

805-648-2075

Index